Cruisin' the 'Nade

Michael R. Halldorson
and David D. Bruhn

In the 1960s, Chico, a northern California college town, offered a unique blend of natural beauty, rich history, and vibrant culture – associated with a regular influx of talent, energy, and enthusiasm – while remaining largely free of big city distractions. The small city grew from 15,000 to 20,000 residents over the decade. Temperate weather combined with outstanding coaches produced many star athletes. Students seeking other types of excitement, could cruise the Esplanade (a stately tree-lined boulevard) in their cars; neck with their dates at the Starlite drive-in theater; or simply enjoy the beauty of Bidwell Park, which stretched miles and miles from downtown to the upper reaches of Big Chico Creek Canyon. Chico State College offered students an inviting environment in which to enjoy social life on and off campus while pursuing their studies. Long known as a party school, *Playboy* magazine ranked it number one in the nation from 1987 through 2002. The city and its college were, however, not completely insulated from the times. In the early '60s, the Air Force built a Titan 1 ballistic missile complex in Chico, believing its site in a rural area would avoid undue attention from the Soviet Union. In the late '60s, an anti-war rally and other unrest occurred on the Chico State campus. Thereafter, for the first time, San Francisco-based bands (reflecting a mixture of Bay Area psychedelics, rock 'n' roll and rebellion) began performing at the school. At decade's end, far from Chico, the famed three-day Woodstock music festival was held on Max Yasgur's dairy farm in Bethel, New York, attended by more than 460,000 young people. Seventy-two photographs and maps add value to this work.

To the scores of former Chico High and Pleasant Valley High School students, and teenagers from smaller, nearby towns venturing to the "big city," who cruised the 'Nade in the '60s, and many decades since to the present.

Cruisin' the 'Nade

Michael R. Halldorson
and David D. Bruhn

HERITAGE BOOKS
2026

HERITAGE BOOKS

AN IMPRINT OF HERITAGE BOOKS, INC.

Books, CDs, and more—Worldwide

For our listing of thousands of titles see our website
at
www.HeritageBooks.com

Published 2026 by
HERITAGE BOOKS, INC.
Publishing Division
5810 Ruatan Street
Berwyn Heights, MD 20740

International Standard Book Number
Paperbound: 978-0-7884-5894-1

Heritage Books by Cdr. David D. Bruhn, USN (Retired)

Battle Stars for the "Cactus Navy":
America's Fishing Vessels and Yachts in World War II

Beavers: American River College's Running Dynasty, 1964–1979
David D. Bruhn and Al Baeta

Cruisin' the 'Nade:
Coming of Age in the 1960s in Northern California
Michael R. Halldorson and David D. Bruhn

Distant Finish
David C. Bruhn and Jack Leydig

Enemy Waters:
Royal Navy, Royal Canadian Navy, Royal Norwegian Navy,
U.S. Navy, and Other Allied Mine Forces Battling the
Germans and Italians in World War II
Cdr. David D. Bruhn, USN (Retired)
and Lt. Cdr. Rob Hoole, RN (Retired)

Eyes of the Fleet:
The U.S. Navy's Seaplane Tenders and
Patrol Aircraft in World War II

Gators Offshore and Upriver:
The U.S. Navy's Amphibious Ships and Underwater Demolition Teams,
and Royal Australian Navy Clearance Divers in Vietnam

Guns Up, Depth Charges Readied:
U.S. Navy, Commonwealth, and Other Allied Escort Ships
Shepherding Convoys, and Battling German and Italian Air
and Naval Forces in the Mediterranean in World War II

Guns Up:
Naval Action in the Yellow Sea off Korea, 1950–1953

Home Waters:
Royal Navy, Royal Canadian Navy, and U.S. Navy
Mine Forces Battling U-Boats in World War I
Cdr. David D. Bruhn, USN (Retired)
and Lt. Cdr. Rob Hoole, RN (Retired)

Ingram's Fourth Fleet:
U.S. and Royal Navy Operations Against German Runners, Raiders,
and Submarines in the South Atlantic in World War II

Intercept:
The U.S. Navy's Intelligence-Gathering Ships
("Cold War Spy Fleet") 1961–1969, 1985–1989

Kissing Cousins:
U.S. Navy Wooden Minesweepers and Variants (YMS, PCS, AGS)
and USN and Royal Australian Navy Bomb and Mine Disposal
Personnel in the Pacific in World War II, 1944–1945

Land Yacht Seaward*:*
Building a Cozy Wooden Camper for a Small Truck

MacArthur and Halsey's "Pacific Island Hoppers":
The Forgotten Fleet of World War II

Nightraiders:
U.S. Navy, Royal Navy, Royal Australian Navy, and Royal Netherlands Navy Mine Forces Battling the Japanese in the Pacific in World War II
Cdr. David D. Bruhn, USN (Retired)
and Lt. Cdr. Rob Hoole, RN (Retired)

On the Gunline:
U.S. Navy and Royal Australian Navy Warships off Vietnam, 1965–1973
Cdr. David D. Bruhn, USN (Retired)
and STGCS Richard S. Mathews, USN (Retired)

Queenstown Bound:
U.S. Navy Destroyers Combating German U-boats in European Waters in World War I

Rarely Idle:
U.S. Navy Sub-chasers and Royal Navy Motor Launches and Canadian-built Drifters Combating German U-boats in World War I
Cdr. David D. Bruhn, USN (Retired),
Lt. Cdr. Rob Hoole, RN (Retired)
and George H. S. Duddy

Ready to Haul, Ready to Fight:
U.S. Navy, Royal Australian Navy, and British Merchant Navy Cargo Ships in the Pacific in World War II

Salvation from the Sky:
U.S. Navy, Royal Australian Air Force, and Royal New Zealand Air Force Heroic Air-Sea Rescue in the Pacific in World War II
Cdr. David D. Bruhn, USN (Retired)
and Stephen Ekholm

Sanctuary Not Certain:
American, British, Australian, and Canadian Hospital Ships in the European–African–Middle Eastern Theatre in World War II

Sandscrapers:
The U.S. Navy's LSMs (Medium Landing Ships) and LSM(R)s (Rocket Ships) in World War II

Send Some King's Ships:
U.S. Navy, Royal Naval Patrol Service, and Royal Canadian Navy Ships Combating German U-boats off North America's Eastern Seaboard, and RNPS and South African Naval Forces Vessels in African Waters as well, 1942–1945
Cdr. David D. Bruhn, USN (Retired)
and Lt. Cdr. Rob Hoole, RN (Retired)

Stand Easy:
Creating a Small British Pub, and Considerable Comradeship, in the Corner of a Garage

Stream Gear:
U.S. Navy, Royal Navy, Royal Australian Navy, South African Naval Forces, and Royal Hellenic Navy Minesweepers' Dangerous Operations in the Mediterranean in World War II.
Cdr. David D. Bruhn, USN (Retired)
and Lt. Cdr. Rob Hoole, RN (Retired)

Stride Out

Support for the Fleet:
U.S. Navy and Royal Australian Navy Service
Force Ships That Served in Vietnam, 1965–1973

Toe the Mark

Turn into the Wind:
Volume I: US Navy and Royal Navy Light Fleet Aircraft Carriers
in World War II, and Contributions of the British Pacific Fleet

Turn into the Wind:
Volume II: US Navy, Royal Navy, Royal Australian Navy, and
Royal Canadian Navy Light Fleet Aircraft Carriers in the
Korean War and through End of Service, 1950–1982

War Bound from Stockton: U.S. Navy Ships from California's
Central Valley, In Harm's Way in Pacific Waters in World War II

We Are Sinking, Send Help!:
The U.S. Navy's Tugs and Salvage Ships in the African,
European, and Mediterranean Theaters in World War II

Wooden Ships and Iron Men:
The U.S. Navy's Coastal and Motor Minesweepers, 1941–1953

Wooden Ships and Iron Men:
The U.S. Navy's Coastal and Inshore Minesweepers, and
the Minecraft that Served in Vietnam, 1953–1976

Wooden Ships and Iron Men:
The U.S. Navy's Ocean Minesweepers, 1953–1994

Heritage Books by Michael R. Halldorson

Cruisin' the 'Nade:
Coming of Age in the 1960s in Northern California
Michael R. Halldorson and David D. Bruhn

Navy Daze:
Coming of Age in the 1960s Aboard a Navy Destroyer

Contents

Foreword by Chuck Sheley xv
Foreword by Sam Simmons xvii
Foreword by Rob Laxson xix
Acknowledgements xxi
Preface xxvii
1. Arrival at Chico High School in 1959 1
2. Major League Pitcher Nelson Briles 5
3. Chico's Cold War Titan 1 Missile Silos 11
4. 1962 State Champion Doug Parker 17
5. Cruisin' and My First Two Cars 23
6. Silver Dollar Speedway 27
7. Active Navy Duty 29
8. Chico High's 1963 Football Team 37
9. Powell Fly Rods 47
10. 1965 Visit Home to Chico 53
11. A Change of Traditional Rivals 57
12. Waning Days Aboard *Hopewell* 63
13. Return to College Life 65
14. Protest Against the Draft in 1968 69
15. Concerts at Chico State in the late 1960s 73
16. Student Body Largely Focused on Studies 79
17. Chico State College's Unconventional Ski Program 83
18. Chico State Boxing 87
Postscript 95
Bibliography/Notes 97
About the Authors 105

Photos

Acknowledgements-1: Chuck Sheley xxii
Acknowledgements-2: Sam Simmons with Coach Willie Simmons xxiii
Acknowledgements-3: Rob Laxson xxiv
Acknowledgements-4: Tim O'Neill xxv
Acknowledgements-5: Bob Hooper xxv
Acknowledgements-6: Lynn Tosello xxvi
Preface-1: Sir Joseph Hooker Oak, circa 1910 xxx
Preface-2: Chico Normal School, founded in 1887 xxxi
Preface-3: Chico High School on the Esplanade xxxii

Preface-4: Chico High School on the Esplanade xxxiii
Preface-5: Wildcat Kim Ellison winning mile race xxxiv
1-1: Chico High School 1
1-2: School monument in front of Chico High School 1
1-3: President John F. Kennedy 2
2-1: Nelson Briles MLB baseball card 5
2-2: Nelson Briles in high school baseball team picture 6
2-3: Nelson Briles in high school play *Damn Yankees* 6
3-1: Sutter Buttes Mountain Range 12
3-2: Titan I missile emerging from its silo at a test facility 12
3-3: Scott Carpenter assisted into his *Aurora 7* spacecraft 14
3-4: Doug Parker in high school basketball team picture 15
4-1: 1962 California State Track and Field Program 17
4-2: Jonathan Peck, Harvard High School half-miler 18
4-3: Two examples of hot rods 22
5-1: Four 1960s Chevrolet model cars 24
5-2: 1953 Chevy 4-door sedan 26
6-1: Sprint car race at the Silver Dollar Speedway 28
7-1: Panorama of Naval Training Station Treasure Island 30
7-2: My '56 Chevy lowly four-door family car 31
7-3: Destroyer USS *Hopewell* at sea during the 1960s 36
8-1: Coaches "Rock" McClellan and "Blackie" Gilbert 38
8-2: Charlie Crabtree, and North-South Shrine Game Press Book 40
8-3: Walton, Press, Rich, and Eugene Powell at the Powell Shop 46
9-1: Press Powell demonstrating fly rod casting techniques 47
9-2: E.C. Powell 48
9-3: Walton Powell with Grayling and Steelhead trout 49
9-4: E.C. Powell and Walton Powell fly rods 49
9-5: College student Press Powell 51
9-6: Twirp King & Queen Reed McLaughlin and Mary Jane Rivers 51
10-1: Vietnam anti-war poster 54
10-2: Pleasant Valley High School 56
11-1: Coaches Mel Jones and "Skip" McDonald 58
11-2: Baseball players "Skip" McDonald and "Bush" Dalrymple 59
11-3: Duwayne Ray and Rob Laxson in mile race 62
12-1: The "Bear Hole" in upper Bidwell Park, Chico 63
13-1: Kendall Hall administration building 65
13-2: Party scene in the late 1960s 67
14-1: Anti-war rally on Chico State campus in 1968 70
14-2: Members of the "Chico 15" seeking to close W. First Street 71
15-1: Singer Lou Rawls 74
15-2: Big Brother and the Holding Company band members 75

15-3: The Grateful Dead band members 76
15-4: Singer Joan Baez 77
15-5: Singers Johnny Cash and Marty Robbins 78
16-1: Little green footbridge over Big Chico Creek 79
16-2: Coach George Maderos 80
16-3: Alpha Phi Omega Fraternity member Mike Halldorson 81
16-4: '57 Chevy 82
17-1: Wildcat ski team member Bob Lockey 83
17-2: Wildcat ski team captain Herb Scott 85
17-3: Chico State ski instructor Garth Dunning 86
18-1: Chico State Boxing team in the early 1970s 87
18-2: Coach Willie Simmons taping the hands of a fighter 88
18-3: Twin brothers Mike and Pat Buzbee 92
18-4: Simmons receiving a desk set from Cal mentor Brian Kahn 93
18-5: Conference Championship individual runner-up trophy 93
18-6: Mike Buzbee handing off to Tracy Smith at the Tahoe Relays 94
18-7: Pat Buzbee finishing the Avenue of the Giants Marathon 94
Postscript-1: Dutch graphic artist M. C. Escher 96
Bibliography/Notes-1: Michael Halldorson's print *Pollution I* 104

Maps

Preface-1: Butte County, California xxvii
4-1: California's CIF Sections 19

Foreword

My memory of Chico in the 1960s comes from the perspective of being a beginning teacher and coach at Chico Junior High School (CJHS). Vietnam dominates, as it affected so many aspects of our lives. Without President Kennedy's change in the draft to defer men with children, I might not be writing this.

Todd Wood was one of my first students at CJHS who was killed in Vietnam. Later, Bill McConnell was one of the best student teachers I ever had out of the 53 that I mentored. Bill was a boxer for Chico State, and we actually put a non-contact boxing unit into our PE program at CJHS. Students loved it. Vice Principal Al Kostiz loved it, as he used our gloves to solve many of the student fights on campus. After ten minutes in the gym with boxing gloves, former enemies left as best friends. Bill was teaching PE in Central California when he was drafted. He went Airborne (82nd), became a medic, and was killed by a sniper with only 30 days left in his tour.

Frank Burk, a Chico State professor, was one of the people who shut down 1st Street to protest the war. He, along with myself, Don Richie, Walt Schafer, and a couple others founded the Chico Running Club.

I was a smokejumper for the U.S. Forest Service in the summer at the time. When we started work in June, I noticed a number of people with great suntans from over the winter. Strange, since they were from Montana. Later, I found out they'd spent part of the winter training Cuban paratroopers in Guatemala for the Bay of Pigs fiasco. What the government does without public knowledge. Little change there.

Chico State boxing was probably the best-attended athletic event in Chico. You had to go early to get a good seat. When NCAA champ Charlie Mohr (University of Wisconsin) died after a match in 1960, boxing remained at just a few schools. Chico State and University of Nevada-Reno were two of those schools. When Nevada came to town, the gym floor was covered with canvas in the seating area to prevent floor damage. Many of the rowdy PE majors like Bob Noe would attend and bang two-by-fours on the floor while chanting, "Enloe! Enloe!" [Reference to local Enloe Hospital.] The Nevada boxers probably thought all the Chico boxers were named "Enloe." The matches were broadcast on local radio.

As a first-year coach, I watched Mel Jones put Doug Parker through repeat 660s prior to the state meet. I attended the state meet in Modesto and saw Doug win the 880. I was sitting next to George Wright. George was one of the Chico State runners who founded the New Ways Athletic Club—part of the counterculture at the time.

Garth Dunning ran an intramural program at Chico State that was outstanding and highly competitive, with a tremendous level of student participation. Since I handled some student teachers, I was considered as staff at Chico State. I entered a teachers' team in the soccer competition—taking myself, Keith Lockwood, Al Holzhey, and John Beck from CJHS, and Garth and Wayne Dawson from Chico State. We won it all. We especially loved beating all the "frat rats."

At least once a month, I would meet with my best friend from my days at Chico High. Stan Statham was changing jobs from the Bank of America to KHSL, where he became a TV anchor. This was before he went into politics and served almost 20 years in the California State Assembly. While "West Side Story" was playing in the background, we tried to solve the problems of the day. Guess we didn't.

A large number of the teachers in the 1960s came from the "Greatest Generation." If there was anything good about World War II, it was the GI Bill, which allowed people to get a college education who could never have done so otherwise. Many of these individuals taught in the Chico Unified School District. Some folks who come to mind: Bill Kemp, Al Crowson, Al Kostiz, Nanette Carter, Willie Simmons, Dottie Collett, Winston Roberts, and more.

Still coaching, I see students on a daily basis during the track season. The athletes are bigger and stronger, but not tougher. PE students seem in a daze as they walk their two warm-up laps while looking at their cell phones.

The 60s were turbulent, but, minus Vietnam, bring it back, please.

Chuck Sheley

Foreword

Chico, the most wonderful place to grow up and grow old. My entire schooling took place in the radius of a square mile—Amer Jay Hamilton, Chico Jr. High, Chico High and Chico State. The instructors were exceptional and molded me by instilling responsibility, toughness, the desire to learn, to get better and to not fear failure.

They gave me the thrill of competing not only on the field, court and track, but most importantly, in the classroom. Looking back, it was they who inspired me to become a teacher and coach and I thank them. Names like Art Acker, Melvin "Bush" Dalrymple, Clifford "Blackie" Gilbert, Gene Howard, Melvin "Mel" Jones, George Maderos, Joseph "Rock" McClellan, Francis "Skip" McDonald, Rex McDougal, Clarence Pentico, Betty Lou Racker, Chuck Sheley, and my father Willie Simmons.

After my excellent education, I had the good fortune to teach and coach in the Chico Unified School District for forty years. With my father teaching and coaching at the University, I have always had a close connection with the institution, especially with the athletic component. I have watched with excitement and wonder as the town grew and became the hub of the North Valley.

Mike and David: this reflection for me (a hometown boy), brought much joy and appreciation for this special place and its gifted people and traditions. Those of you who have and continue to "cruise The 'Nade," enjoy and remember.

Sam ("Sambo") Simmons

Foreword

One of the wonderful things about growing up in a small town is the unlimited opportunity to be able to participate in a whole host of sports offered by the city as well as local schools. The town of Chico, California, in the 1950s, 1960s and 1970s, was just such a place. Located ninety miles north of the capital of Sacramento—with a population of a little over 12,000 in 1950—Chico was the largest city between Sacramento and the Oregon border.

Whether it was recreational, interscholastic, or intercollegiate sports, Chico and its schools offered young students an opportunity to participate and distinguish themselves within the community at large. Because of its "large" population in this region of the state, Chico teams were often the real "powerhouses" in sports. The local newspaper, *Chico Enterprise-Record*, had an excellent sports department which featured the local teams and athletes and their accomplishments.

With the backdrop of society's turbulent 1960s, the community embraced these sports programs cheering on their teams and individuals. This book is a very thorough chronicle of those sports teams and individual "stars," and is an enjoyable read for any sports fan. The authors have researched and compiled a history of local Chico athletes and their sports with individual statistics, while they were attending Chico's two high schools or Chico State College (now California State University, Chico). They offer these sports memories, while reminding the reader of the anti-establishment events happening at that time in Chico that were intertwined with America's history, giving the book a real depth of facts of that era not often found in other books on the subject.

Rob Laxson

Acknowledgements

The street is the river of life of the city, the place where we come together, the pathway to the center.

—William H. Whyte

Many thanks to Debbie Riley, Heritage Books editor and book designer, for her superlative cover art. The Chico High School and Chico State College letterman jackets serving as the backdrop on the front and back covers belong to co-author David Bruhn and 1967 Chico State graduate Robert Hooper, respectively.

A number of years ago, I met Bruhn, a retired Navy commander who had returned to Chico, a hometown we share. Upon learning that he had authored several books on naval history, I asked him if he would help me with a manuscript I'd written about my time aboard the USS *Hopewell* in the mid-1960s. He readily agreed and the resultant book, *Navy Daze, Coming of Age in the 1960s Aboard a Navy Destroyer*, was published by Heritage Books in 2016.

After beginning this book detailing the trials and tribulations associated with passage through high school and college, I again sought his assistance. I graduated from Chico High School in 1961 and he in 1975. We shared many similar experiences and both have a deep love for Chico. We agreed to collaborate, with me concentrating on the journey itself, and Bruhn researching and writing about people and topics that would increase the book's depth and breadth. It's our hope that *CRUISIN' THE 'NADE* will resonate with both readers from Chico and those with shared experiences in towns and cities from surrounding areas.

The book's title is actually a teenager "shorthand" referring to the 1960s practice of cruising the Esplanade (a boulevard in Chico) into the downtown area, looking for excitement. Many stately homes lined this north-south thoroughfare and their owners did not particularly welcome a parade of cars by their domiciles Friday and Saturday nights.

The expression *Cruisin' the 'Nade* also applies generally to high school and college students seeking excitement and adventure in a variety of ways at night and on the weekends following their dutiful weekday toil in claustrophobic classrooms.

FOREWORD WRITERS

I am very grateful to Chuck Sheley, Sam Simmons, and Rob Laxson for penning forewords offering their unique perspective on the 1960s. Outstanding high school and college athletes, they each chose to become teachers and coaches, heir apparent to predecessors highlighted in this book who influenced and guided them.

Chuck Sheley

Chuck Sheley is a legendary figure in the world of running in northern California, and rightly so. His career teaching PE at Chico Junior High School and coaching track and cross country at Chico High School lasted more than four decades, during which he touched the lives of thousands of students and student athletes, in and out of the classroom.

Sheley lettered in track (4 times) and cross country (1 time) the initial season when Dr. Don Adee established cross country at Chico State. He ran a 49.2 second quarter mile while a college athlete in his senior year at Chico State in 1960. He competed in the NAIA national championships his freshman year, and the equivalent of today's Division II the remaining three years.

Concurrently with teaching, Sheley was a smokejumper for the U.S. Forest Service for eight seasons in Oregon and four seasons for the Bureau of Land Management (BLM) in Alaska.

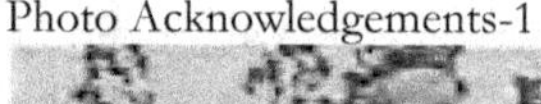
Photo Acknowledgements-1

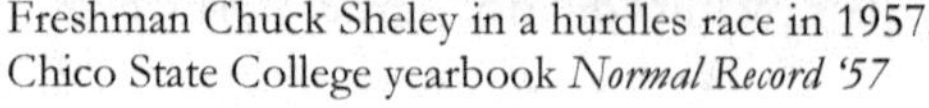
Freshman Chuck Sheley in a hurdles race in 1957.
Chico State College yearbook *Normal Record '57*

Chuck Sheley is a member of the Chico State Athletic Hall of Fame, *Chico Enterprise-Record* Sports Hall of Fame and, in 2025, was inducted into the Chico High Sports Boosters Hall of Fame inaugural class.

Sam Simmons

Photo Acknowledgements-2

Wildcat boxer Sam Simmons getting advice from his coach (and father) Willie Simmons during his bout at a 1967 match against University of Nevada-Reno in Chico's Acker Gym. He was advised, "Keep your hands up and circle away from the power!!!" "Keep Busy!" Simmons, wearing 12 oz. gloves and headgear, fought at the 139 or 147 lb. weight class. The boxing ring mat was padded and the ropes were tight and padded for safety.
Courtesy of Sam Simmons

Sam Simmons lettered in football, basketball, and track at Chico High. He was a four-sport athlete at Chico State, earning seven letters: football (2 years), boxing (3 years), track (1 year), and soccer (1 year). Simmons was the Art Acker Distinguished Athlete in 1969—the same recognition his father Willie Simmons received in 1950. Also, like his father, Sam was student body president at Chico State, and joined him in the Chico State Athletic and *Chico Enterprise-Record* Sports Halls of Fame.

Simmons did his student teaching in 1970 for "Skip" McDonald, during summer school at Chico High School. He recalled about this experience, these were "fifty young men who had failed PE; I learned a lot!" After bouncing around between area schools for several years, the opportunity came to return to his alma mater in 1991 when McDonald retired. Thereafter, Simmons was Chico High's head basketball coach and taught PE until his retirement in 2009.

Rob Laxson

An outstanding high school and college athlete, and later a lauded coach, Rob Laxson is featured in Chapter 11, titled "A Change of Traditional Rivals." Until the mid-1960s, Chico High was a dominant powerhouse in northern California, with a proud tradition of excellence in many areas including sports. That changed with the establishment of Pleasant Valley High School (PV) in Chico, which diluted that power. The presence of a second high school also set up a crosstown rivalry between Chico and PV that continues to the present.

One of the stellar student athletes who went from Chico High to PV was Laxson—a product of a community whose spirit, culture, and abundant opportunity to engage in a variety of sports produced many "greats."

Photo Acknowledgements-3

At a track meet against UC Davis in 1970, Wildcat Rob Laxson (center) and teammate Jim Estes, coming up on his outside in the homestretch to draw even, finished the hotly contested half-mile race in a tie for first-place.
Courtesy of Jim Estes

OTHER CONTRIBUTORS

Photo Acknowledgements-4

Photo Acknowledgements-5

Left: 1963 Chico High Football team running back Tim O'Neill.
Right: 1966 Chico State Cross Country team member Bob Hooper.
Chico High School yearbook *Caduceus '64*
Chico State College yearbook *Record '67*

I am very appreciative of Tim O'Neill providing details about the Chico High School 1963-64 school year football team, of which he was a member, and remembrances he shared of good friend Press Powell. O'Neill served with the 199th infantry in Vietnam. Afterward, he attended college, then law school, becoming an attorney and owner of a law firm.

As mentioned earlier, Bob Hooper graciously lent his Chico State College letterman's jacket for cover art backdrop. "Hoop," a retired Army Physician Assistant (CW4, USA), remains involved with running sports through his duties as a Master Level USA Track & Field Umpire at Cross Country and Track Meets. Much earlier in the 1960s and 70s, Bob was a firefighter for the California Division of Forestry (6 seasons), then became a smokejumper for BLM in Alaska (2 seasons) and out of Cave Junction, Oregon (7 seasons)—159 jumps in total.

Much information and photographs used in the book came from the Chico State student newspaper *Wildcat* (later renamed *Orion*) and Chico State *Record* student yearbooks. I am grateful to the California State University, Chico Meriam Library Special Collections and University Archives for allowing their use, and to Ryan Browar, who assisted me in making this possible.

Many thanks to Mike Wolcott and Justin Couchot, editor and sports reporter for the *Chico Enterprise-Record*, respectively, for their interest in and support of this book, which included allowing the use of photographs and material from the 1960s.

Rich Morrison kindly provided Powell family photographs and information used in Chapter 9, titled Powell Fly Rods. Morrison is the webmaster of Classic Powell Rod (https://classicpowellrod.com/).

Other contributors of materials and/or photographs used include twins Mike and Pat Buzbee, Bob Darling, Scott Fairley, brothers Bill and Rich Gregg, Hank Lawson, Joe Mangan, and Susan St. Germaine.

Finally, David Bruhn and I am very appreciative of the efforts of editor Lynn Tosello—a 1973 graduate of Pleasant Valley High School. In addition to knowledge of prose, syntax, and other such things that one would expect of an English major, she also brought a critical eye, judicious pen, flair, and understanding of subject matter to this project. Progressing through secondary school in Chico, Lynn has a foot in each camp. She attended Bidwell Junior High whose graduating freshmen, like those of Chico Junior High, moved on to PV or Chico High. She went to PV, whereas former classmates who resided further west in the community, thereafter trod the halls of Chico High.

Photo Acknowledgements-6

1980 Chico State University graduation Lynn Tosello.
Courtesy of Lynn Tosello

Preface

Towns change; they grow or diminish, but hometowns remain as we left them.

—Jayne Anne Phillips

City life is millions of people being lonesome together.

—Henry David Thoreau

GROWING UP IN CHICO IN THE 1960s WAS GREAT FUN. Before delving into proof of this declaration in the body of this book, it's appropriate to "set the table" so to speak, regarding why Chico was, and remains today, a special place. This short introduction provides an overview of both Chico and Butte County where the city is located in northern California.

Map Preface-1

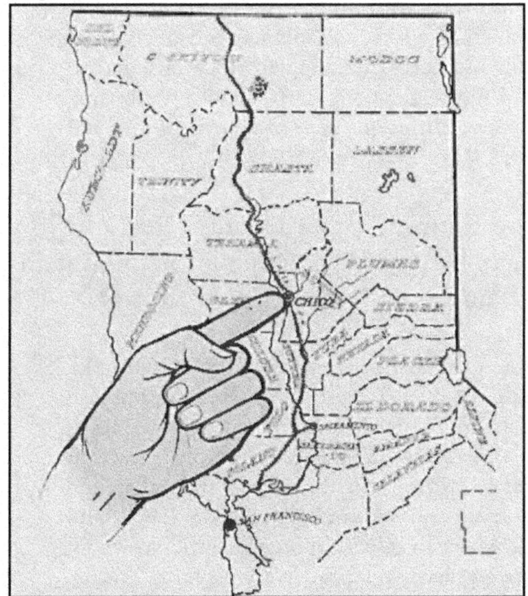

Chico, California: A Pamphlet, Chico Chamber of Commerce, Briscoe-Nash Publishing Co., 1904 (http://archives.csuchico.edu/digital/collection/coll24/id/1519/rec/4: accessed 2 January 2026)

BUTTE COUNTY

A promotional booklet titled *Butte County, California* by the Chico Chamber of Commerce, Oroville Chamber of Commerce, Gridley Chamber of Commerce, Biggs Chamber of Commerce, Paradise Progressive Association, Durham Business Men's Association and Richvale Farm Center, published in 1922, describes the creation, early development and geography of the county.

> Containing 1764 square miles of territory, Butte County, California, is located in the northeastern part of the State, in the northern and eastern part of the great interior Sacramento Valley. The county is approximately 200 miles north of the city of San Francisco, and 100 miles north of Sacramento, the State Capital.
>
> Butte County was one of the first nineteen counties created when California was organized in 1850, although the territory then embraced was much larger than it is now. As population grew other counties were carved from its territory, but it still remains geographically as large as several of the eastern States.
>
> The lands of Butte County, generally speaking, can be divided into three parts: the mountain lands, where abound a wealth of timber and minerals and water power; the foothill lands, rolling, sparsely wooded, many square miles of which are adapted and devoted to citrus and deciduous fruit and berry growing and stock raising; and the valley lands, level and fertile, devoted to fruit and nut growing, grains, rice, hay and many different lines of horticulture and agriculture.[1]

As highlighted in the booklet, Butte County's early history involved a dramatic transition from goldmining in the mountains to farming in the foothills and valley areas of the county.

> In the pioneer days, when men rushed westward in search of gold, the foothills and mountains of Butte County were scenes of feverish activity. The rivers and streams were rich in gold and roaring camps were on every slope. The era of mining passed from placer to hydraulic to deep gravel to quartz. In those days the valley and foothill lands were largely untenanted and unworked. Large land grants, dating back to the Mexican rule, shut out the settler in search of small acreage and were given over principally to cattle raising. Few of the pioneers came to California to farm. The gold mines were the goal and practically all of them dreamed of a "stake" and a return to the east.

> But it was not a great while before the decline of the mining era set in. Many who mined were not successful in any degree, and among these virile young pioneers were those from the farms of the east and middle west. They had been reared on farms and they knew good lands and saw in the foothill and valley parts of the county an opportunity to acquire homesites and valuable property, and they turned away from the mountains and towards the low lands.
>
> With the decline of mining and the exhaustion of the placers this movement was augmented. Population steadily decreased in the mountains and grew in the valleys and foothills. Government lands, where available, were pre-empted, and the Mexican grants subdivided by their owners for settlement.... Towns and cities were founded with resources back of them more enduring than the transitory lure of gold. The railroads came, highways were built, schools and churches founded. Soon the incomparable climate, the fertile soil, the diversity of products which were possible, created a prosperous, growing commonwealth, with flourishing towns and villages....[2]

The population of Butte County at the census of 1920 was 30,030. This population was well distributed through the foothill and valley sections, predominately in the latter. The population of the mountain sections was largely seasonal and transient, although there were many permanent residents with homes, orchards, mines and stock ranges.[3]

CITY OF CHICO

Chico, located in the northwestern end of the county, ninety miles north of Sacramento, is the largest city in Butte County. It was founded in 1860 by John Bidwell, illustrious California pioneer, who came to the state before the discovery of gold. Following his finding of gold, he used his new wealth to acquire a Mexican grant of 26,000 acres which he farmed on an extensive scale and pioneered the planting of orchards in this part of the valley. Following the death of General Bidwell in 1900, subdivision of the greater part of his ranch occurred and rapid growth of the city ensued.[4]

The booklet *Butte County, California*, described the City of Chico in 1922, and its attractions cited remain today.

> Situated as it is in the center of one of the richest agricultural districts of California, it has become commercially and in population the largest city in the central part of California north of Sacramento [and remains so today]. The city is surrounded by productive orchards of prunes, peaches, almonds, cherries, and other fruits and

nuts. It is one of the chief centers of the almond growing industry of California, while its production of prunes runs into the thousands of tons.

The tree growth in and around Chico is the most remarkable in California. Trees and shrubs from all the climes of the world grow and flourish throughout its magnificent park, the third largest in the world.

Comprising 2,400 acres, the native oaks grow to astounding size, and one of them, the Sir Joseph Hooker Oak, is declared to be the largest and most symmetrical in the world. This park, given to the city by General and Mrs. Bidwell, has been preserved in all its primitive beauty, and is being developed by the municipality with golf links, bath houses and natural pools, drives, and other recreational facilities, all free to the public.

Photo Preface-1

Postcard of the landmark Sir Joseph Hooker Oak, circa 1910.

Bidwell Park, one of the crown jewels of Chico, is no longer claimed as the third largest in the world, but remains one of the largest municipal parks in the United States. The greatly beloved Hooker Oak was felled by a windstorm on May 1, 1977. Upon first seeing the massive Valley Oak in 1872, the English botanist Sir Joseph Dalton Hooker declared it to be largest of its species in the known world. Stretching upward 105 feet in height, at its demise the tree was 326 years old; the circumference of its trunk was 28 feet and that of the outside branches nearly five hundred feet. The shaded area under the tree's expansive foliage was 18,000 square feet.[5]

In 1922, Chico was known as the City of Parks, for in addition to Bidwell Park, it had a beautiful children's playground, a city plaza, and two other improved parks, all open to the public at all times. (Today, Chico is referred to as the City of Trees.) The population of Chico was then about 12,000 within the city limits.[6]

NORTHERN CALIFORNIA EDUCATIONAL CENTER

Photo Preface-2

Chico Normal School, founded in 1887. In the decades that followed, the school greatly expanded and was sequentially renamed Chico State Teachers College, later Chico State College, and finally California State University, Chico.
The Normal Record Volume I, March, 1896
(http://archives.csuchico.edu/digital/collection/coll4/id/11561/rec/15: accessed 1 January 2026).

At this time (1920s), Chico was also known as the educational center of northern California [excluding, of course, the San Francisco Bay Area which boasted UC Berkeley and Stanford Universities. These premiere schools were founded in 1868 and 1885, respectively].

As noted in the 1922 booklet *Butte County, California*:

> Here is located the Chico State Teachers College, an institution for the training of teachers, with a large enrollment; a new one-million-dollar high school, a complete business college, and a primary and

grammar school system of wide extent. Many families move to Chico solely for its educational advantages.[7]

The founding of Chico Normal School occurred in 1887, when General John Bidwell donated eight acres of his cherry orchard on the southern side of Big Chico Creek to establish the Northern Branch State Normal School of California. The school officially opened in 1889 with 90 students and five faculty members. It became Chico State Teachers College in 1921. In 1935 a legislative act changed the college name from Chico State Teachers College to Chico State College, and in 1972, Chico State College became California State University, Chico. Alumni and current students still commonly refer to their school as "Chico State."

Vintage Chico State Wildcat Logo.[8]

CHICO HIGH SCHOOL

Photo Preface-3

Chico High School on the Esplanade. The original high school on West First Street was destroyed by fire in January 1911.
Chico, California: A Pamphlet, Chico Chamber of Commerce, Briscoe-Nash Publishing Co., 1904 (http://archives.csuchico.edu/digital/collection/coll24/id/1519/rec/4: accessed 2 January 2026)

Chico High School (CHS) was established on April 19, 1902, and began its first session on September 2, when its principal, William M. Mackay, introduced himself and his faculty to the 46 students. For its first few years, classes met on the third floor of the old Oakdale School. In April, 1905, Chico High School moved to its first "permanent" building—an elegant Grecian style edifice on West First Street, surrounded by grand old cherry trees on three-and-a-half acres purchased out of the famed Bidwell cherry orchard.[9]

When fire destroyed the original Chico High School building in January, 1911, classes met in the Presbyterian Church for the remainder of the school year. (The former CHS site is the present site of the Chico State Meriam Library). Accompanied by ceremonies and celebration, October 1, 1920, marked the laying of the cornerstone of a new CHS campus (at its current site) 300 feet back from the Esplanade. Nineteen months later on April 28, 1922, the entire student body and faculty moved from the old campus to the newly completed site.[10]

Photo Preface-4

Chico High School on the Esplanade, 1925. Snowfall is rare in Chico. The Esplanade boulevard is the main north-south thoroughfare in Chico.
Photo from Meriam Library Special Collections.

Chico State and Chico High were then, and remain today, closely linked owing to education and proximity; parts of the two campuses face each other across Warner Street. This street was named after Warner Brothers Studio. In recognition of the beauty of Bidwell Park, which stretches miles and miles from downtown to the upper reaches of Chico Creek Canyon, a studio crew ventured 500 miles north from Hollywood in 1938 to film "The Adventures of Robin Hood" (a motion picture starring Errol Flynn) in Chico's "Sherwood Forest."

CHICO'S FRIENDLY ATMOSPHERE ATTRACTS WEEKENDERS, OTHER VISITORS, COLLEGE STUDENTS, AND RESIDENTS

Wildcat Track & Field

Photo Preface-5

Kim Ellison winning the mile race during a home meet on April 29, 1972. *Chico Enterprise-Record*

In 1972, while a Chico State student and Wildcat athlete, Kim Ellison ran a 4:01 mile and earned All-American honors. When asked what had drawn him, a former southern California high school track star, to the small college and small town in the northern end of the Sacramento Valley—which didn't even offer athletic scholarships—he explained:

> I first set foot on the Chico State campus in the Spring of 1964. My English teacher and cross country coach the previous Fall, Jim Roulsten, brought three teammates and myself from the San Fernando Valley north to Chico. As the former Student Body President at Chico State and one of its most vocal off-campus cheerleaders, Coach Roulsten wanted to show us his old alma mater. We met the then track coach (and legendary coach of everything) Willie Simmons. We strolled down 1st Street that had great old Victorian homes (mostly fraternity and sorority houses) staring right across the street at what is now the administrative building. We were continually STUNNED by countless people passing by on campus and in town who often waved to us and said, "Hello," or "Good morning." I remember asking Coach Roulsten, "Do you know these people?" His response was, "No. We're in Chico." Add to those friendly folk the beauty of Bidwell Park, the almond trees in blossom, Chico Creek meandering through a storybook college campus.
>
> I knew I'd be back.[11]

1

Arrival at Chico High School in 1959

When I was 5 years old, my mother always told me that happiness was the key to life. When I went to school, they asked me what I wanted to be when I grew up. I wrote down 'happy'. They told me I didn't understand the assignment, and I told them they didn't understand life.

—John Lennon.

Photo 1-1

Chico High School.
Butte County, California
Chico Chamber of Commerce, Chico, Cal. ... et al, 1922

Photo 1-2

Monument displaying the pride and determination of the school.
Chico High School yearbook *Caduceus '60*

My "coming of age" began in September 1959 when I, and other Chico Junior High School graduates, moved on to Chico High School to begin our sophomore year. It ended in June 1969 upon my graduation from Chico State College. A three-year hitch in the Navy in the mid-1960s, serving aboard a destroyer off the coast of the Republic of Vietnam, marked an interlude in my studies at Chico State.

The 1960s started off with most Americans anticipating the dawn of a golden age. On January 20, 1961, youthful, charismatic John F. Kennedy (JFK) became president of the United States. However, the expected golden age never materialized. By the end of the 1960s, there was much more strife and turmoil than when the decade began.

Photo 1-3

President John F. Kennedy welcomes the Coast Guard sail training ship USCGC *Eagle* to the Washington Navy Yard, August 1962. Naval History and Heritage Command photograph #NH 93372

The failed Bay of Pigs invasion (April 1961) and subsequent Cuban Missile Crisis (October 1962) were disasters for JFK. Kennedy was assassinated in November 1963, upon which Vice President Lyndon B. Johnson assumed the presidency.

Johnson's administration was marked by Great Society programs, reflecting a broader commitment to social justice and equality, including the Civil Rights Act of 1964 and the Voting Rights Act of 1965. It was was also characterized by the Vietnam War, which faced significant domestic opposition. Johnson decided not to run for a second term in 1968, marking the end of his presidency.

Richard M. Nixon became president in January 1969, having promised to guide America out of the Vietnam War by pursuing a policy of "peace with honor" (the withdrawal of American forces from Vietnam in a way that avoided any appearance of defeat).

At decade's end, as the war in Vietnam continued, shreds of the hopeful '60s remained. In the summer of 1969, the Woodstock Music and Art Fair was held on Max Yasgur's dairy farm in Bethel, New York. Billed as "an Aquarian Exposition: 3 Days of Peace & Music," more than 460,000 young people attended the Woodstock music festival.

I had no inkling of what the future held when I walked wide-eyed through the front door of Chico High in autumn 1959. As a high school student in the late '50s and early '60s, I was completely naïve about world affairs and did not realize that actions were taking place in Southeast Asia that would directly affect my life a few years later.[1]

COMING OF AGE BEGINS WITH DRIVER'S LICENSE

In Chico in the 1950s, when not attending school, kids spent most of their waking hours outdoors, riding their bikes, playing sports, or doing chores such as mowing the lawn. The (mostly) black & white televisions in homes could only pick up two local stations, channels 7 and 12, on their antennas. Children watched cartoons on Saturday morning and sometimes shows in the evenings. Parent choices (beginning with the news) dictated what was on during primetime viewing. Indoor kid entertainment was otherwise largely playing board games with siblings.

After passing into high school at age 15, a few of my fellow sophomores aspired from day one to attend great colleges, and studied hard to achieve top marks. Others muddled through classes while dreaming of getting their driver's license as a prerequisite to gaining a measure of independence, and ability to take a member of the opposite sex on a date. Ideally, your parents would allow you to use the family car; if not, you could try to get an afterschool and/or weekend job, in order to save enough to buy a used one.

I was part of the latter group. My most exciting times at Chico High School involved cars and girls—a continuing theme during my 1960s decade-long "coming of age." My experiences are interspersed throughout the book with sketches of some great Chico High athletes who wore the red and gold school colors. Growing up I, like many other boys, played football, basketball and baseball with other kids in pickup games on playgrounds or in organized team leagues such as Pop Warner football or Little League. Many future Chico High star athletes emerged from such activities. I did not play high school sports, but I enjoyed sports and appreciated those who excelled at them.

I did not personally know every one of the half-dozen or so athletes I highlight in the book. But I was either aware of their great successes in the 1960s, or have learned about them since then and admire their achievements. Many of these "Chico Greats" are no longer with us, having "crossed the bar" (passed away). They represented Chico extremely well, and deserve a little more "time in the sun" so to speak.

MLB PITCHER NELSON BRILES

One such was Nelson Briles, arguably the finest athlete to be produced by Chico in the 1960s. The young Nelson started with a 90-92 mph fastball and in 1965 he made it to the "Big Leagues" (Major League Baseball) as a pitcher.

My only connection to Nelson in school was that I had the dubious notoriety of being hit in the face by a volleyball during a game of dodgeball in a junior high PE class. At Chico Junior High on rainy days, we played "Bombardment" (dodgeball). On one of these days, as was the convention, two groups of male students were formed side-by-side on each side of the gym with volleyballs used as weapons.

One of our PE teachers was standing next to me and noticed Nelson taking aim at him. As Nelson wound up to throw the ball diagonally from quite some distance away, this teacher quickly stepped behind me, lifted me off the floor and used me as a shield. The rest is history. I have not named the teacher. I don't know what the statute of limitations is—but I don't want him arrested.

FAMOUS FRIENDS AND ACQUAINTANCES

In November 2020, Country singers Chris Young and Kane Brown released a popular song titled Famous Friends. Its lyrics include:

> I've got some famous friends
> You probably never heard of
> But back in Rutherford County
> Our crowd is second to none
> You might not know 'em here
> In this big city we're in
> But when I go back home
> I got some famous friends

This song celebrates the friendships and connections that people have in their hometowns, highlighting the camaraderie and recognition of local fame, which this book also endeavors to do.

2

Major League Pitcher Nelson Briles

If what you did yesterday still looks good to you today, then you haven't done anything today.

—Remark made by former major league infielder and Phillies scout Eddie Bockman to Nelson Briles.

Nelson Briles will be remembered as a good ballplayer; a good front-office man and simply a good guy.

—*Pittsburgh-Post Gazette* 2005 editorial following the passing of Briles at age 61 on February 14, 2005.

Photo 2-1

Professional Baseball Career

Pitched for two National League teams:

- St. Louis Cardinals (six years)
- Pittsburgh Pirates (three years)

Pitched for three American League teams:

- Kansas City Royals (two years)
- Texas Rangers, (two years)
- Baltimore Orioles (parts of two years)

Nelson Kelley Briles was born on August 5, 1943, in the very small town of Dorris, located in northern California between Mount Shasta and the Oregon border on U.S. Route 97. Dorris had a population of 810 in the most recent census data of 2023.[1]

Both parents worked in the lumber industry. His father as a general mechanic, his mother caught and sorted boards ("pulled green chain") as they were sawed. Frequent relocation requirements accompanied these jobs; Briles estimated his family moved about 40 times during his youth. Throughout this turbulence, his parents made sure that he had continued access to baseball.[2]

At Chico High School, Briles was a three-sport athlete—football, basketball, and baseball. He was a T-Formation quarterback and the team punter, played varsity basketball, and pitched for the baseball team. When not pitching, he played third base. "Nellie" also took part in school plays. While starring in the lead role of *Damn Yankees*, he met his high school sweetheart, Ginger Moore, whom he married in 1965.[3]

Photo 2-2

Photo 2-3

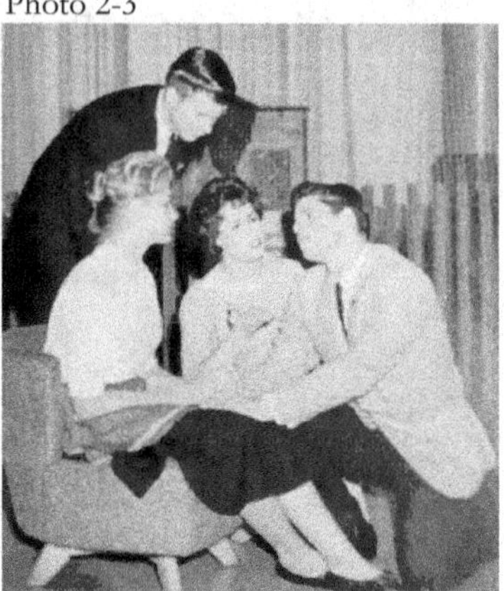

Top left: Nelson Briles pictured in a portion of the Chico High School Varsity Baseball team photograph. Right: Members of the cast of the play *Damn Yankees*.
L-R: Bob Fry, Lynn Tranthem, Kathie Kempton, Nelson Briles.
Chico High School yearbooks *Caduceus '60* and *Caduceus '61*

Graduating high school in 1961, Briles accepted a baseball scholarship to Santa Clara University. He had an 11-2 pitching record his freshman year and, over the summer, pitched semi-pro baseball in Canada for the Medicine Hat, Alberta, team. He went 16-4 and thoroughly enjoyed the experience except when plying his trade in the home ballpark. Sited along a river, it hosted the biggest and most numerous bugs anywhere. Nelson recalled:

> That's the only place I know where the game had to be interrupted because of bugs. So many bugs swarmed over the lights that the bulbs would pop. The lights had to be turned off for a while in hopes the bugs would go away.[4]

Nelson returned to Santa Clara University that fall. During the school year, his family suffered an unexpected loss when his father, Ray, passed away due to a heart attack. Subsequently, family members celebrated Nelson being signed by the St. Louis Cardinals to a contract with an estimated bonus of $40,000-$50,000. He helped his mother pay off medical bills and get a car so she could return to work, and assisted his older twin brothers to fund junior college educations.[5]

BRILES MAKES IT TO "THE SHOW" IN 1965

While playing Minor League "Double A" ball for the Cardinals' Tulsa Oilers affiliate in the Texas League, Briles attended Chico State College in both autumn 1964 and 1965, primarily to be with Ginger. Because he received a signing bonus in 1964, major league baseball required that the Cardinals put Briles on their 1965 major league roster or risk losing him to another team in the first-year draft. St. Louis protected Briles, and called him up to "the Bigs" (Big Leagues).[6]

St. Louis manager (Albert Fred) "Red" Schoendienst initially used Nelson as a "mop-up man" (long reliever). A long reliever is a relief pitcher who is expected to pitch more innings per appearance than other relievers. Typically, a long reliever is sent in when the starting pitcher is struggling early in the game, or when the manager wishes to conserve the arms of other relievers. Commonly, this duty involved pitching the last few innings of a game in which one team had an insurmountable lead.[7]

Briles' first major league appearance came in a mid-April game against the Chicago Cubs. His first major league victory was in relief against the San Francisco Giants in early July. Briles ended up with 37 appearances during the 1965 season, 35 were in relief. He finished the season with a 3-3 record and four saves, and a 3.50 earned run average (ERA).[8]

Skipping ahead two years, Nelson began the Cardinal 1967 season as strictly a relief pitcher. Red made Nelson a starting pitcher after ace Bob Gibson suffered a broken leg. Briles made one more relief appearance, before being moved into the starting rotation for the rest of the season. He ended with a 14-5 record with a 2.43 ERA—the highest winning percentage (.737) in the National League.[9]

CARDINALS WIN THE 1967 WORLD SERIES

Without Nellie there's no way we would have won the pennant that year.

—Cardinal teammate Dal Maxvill.

The Cardinals played the Boston Red Sox in the 1967 World Series, winning it four games to three. Nelson started Game 3 in St. Louis, in the Cardinals' new Busch Memorial Stadium. All of his family came from California to watch him pitch. They didn't have a lot of money, so they stayed with Nelson and Ginger. Briles later mused about the night preceding his appearance, "I'm starting a World Series game, the first one in my life, and I am sleeping on the floor of the living room so my mother could have a bed."[10]

No matter. Briles pitched a 5-2 win in Game 3, allowing seven hits and no walks by batters. He also pitched in relief in Game 6. The Cardinals were losing 4-2 in the sixth and Nelson pitched two shutout innings. For the World Series, he compiled a 1-0 record and posted a 1.64 ERA in 11 innings pitched.[11]

Reflecting later on the Cardinals victory, Briles said:

> You realize you are the world champions that you've won the World Series but the importance of that doesn't really sink in until you've had a chance to think about it over the winter. And you hear people talk about it and how special it is, and how few people are able to enjoy that as a player. And what a special relationship for the players on the team and the fans, and the character of the club, the blended talent, is something that a lot of teams never capture. And the luster of that memory continues to grow, and it was something in your life that can never be taken away. You were on a team that was so special for that frozen moment in time.[12]

CARDINALS UNABLE TO REPEAT IN 1968

The 1968 World Series pitted the Cardinals against the Detroit Tigers. The Tigers won this series 4-3, a great disappointment to the Cardinals as a team and Briles individually. He finished the 1968 World Series with a 0-1 record and a 5.56 ERA in 11 1/3 innings pitched. Briles later lamented the Cardinals led the Series 3-1 after four games and still lost:

> That's one of those things that are still hard to swallow. We had back-to-back world championships within our reach, and it slipped through our fingers.[13]

TRADE TO THE PITTSBURGH PIRATES

In early 1971, the Cardinals traded Briles to the Pittsburgh Pirates. He ended his 6-year career with St. Louis with a 61-54 record and a 3.42 ERA. In his 234 appearances, Briles pitched 116 games in relief and 118 games as a starter, totaling 969 2/3 innings with the Cardinals.[14]

1971 WORLD SERIES AGAINST BALTIMORE

With the 1971 World Series tied at 2-2, Pirates' manager Danny Murtaugh chose Nelson to start Game 5 against the Orioles. Briles pitched his best game of his season, a 5-0 shutout allowing only two hits and walking two. At bat, Nelson also got a key single, driving in one of the Pirates' four runs. The Pirates went on to win the Series 4-3.[15]

TRADE TO THE KANSAS CITY ROYALS

In December 1973, the Pirates traded Briles to the Kansas City Royals. He began the 1974 season as a starting pitcher, but suffered a series of knee injuries and finished with 18 appearances, 103 innings pitched, a record of 5-7, and a 4.02 ERA.[16]

In 1975, Briles suffered an elbow injury which resulted in another disappointing season. The Royals were 15-9 when Nelson played, and he played more than the previous season, but had only 24 appearances, with 112 innings pitched, a 6-6 record and a 4.26 ERA.[17]

TRADE TO THE TEXAS RANGERS

In early November 1975, the Royals traded Nelson Briles to the Texas Rangers. He began the 1976 season as a starting pitcher, and had his best season in recent years. Honored at a Ranger Winter Banquet as the team's "Pitcher of the Year," he appeared in 32 games, pitched 210 innings, and posted an 11-9 record with a 3.26 ERA.[18]

TRADE TO THE BALTIMORE ORIOLES

Briles began 1977 with the Rangers and ended up with the Orioles. He finished the season with a 6-4 record and a 4.33 ERA. In 1978, Nelson started eight times and relieved eight times for the Orioles. He pitched 54 1/3 innings and finished with a 4.64 ERA in posting a 4-4 record.

The Orioles released Briles in January 1979, following which he spent spring training with the New York Mets. Nelson did not win a roster spot and did not pitch Major League Baseball again.[19]

CAREER STATISTICS

Over his 14-year major league career, Briles posted a 129-112 record with a career 3.44 earned run average. He appeared in 452 games and pitched 2,111 2/3 innings.[20]

POST-BASEBALL CAREER WORK

Nelson Briles quickly began his post-baseball career in Pittsburgh doing part-time television analysis for the Pirates. From 1981-1983, he provided analysis for the Game of the Week broadcast on the USA Cable Network, and subsequently worked three years broadcasting Seattle Mariners games.[21]

Briles became a full-time Pirate employee in 1986 working as Director of Corporate Sales, then became a vice president of Corporate Projects. These projects included running the Pirates alumni association.

Nelson Briles was inducted into the *Chico Enterprise-Record* Sports Hall of Fame in 1984, the Pennsylvania State Sports Hall of Fame in 1994, and most recently was posthumously inducted at the inaugural Chico High Sports Boosters Hall of Fame dinner in autumn 2025.[22]

Sadly, Briles died at age 61 of a heart attack on February 14, 2005, as he played in the annual Pirates alumni golf tournament.[23]

3

Chico's Cold War Titan 1 Missile Silos

Returning to the early 1960s, while Nelson, I and fellow high school students were engrossed in our daily lives, the U.S. Defense Department built a "Cold War" missile base in our small rural town.

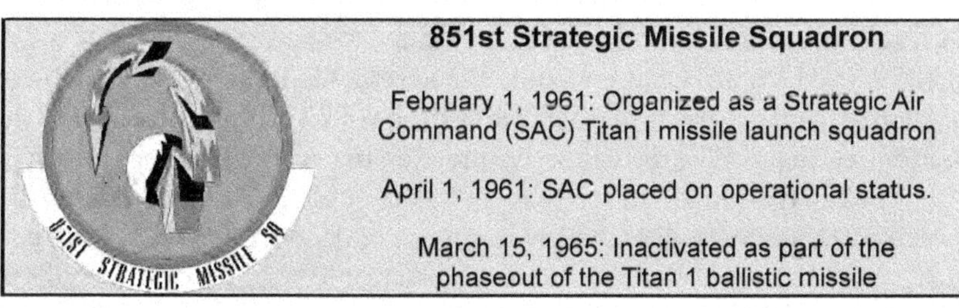

Beale Air Force Base (70 miles south-southeast of Chico) was home in the early 1960s to the 851st Strategic Missile Squadron, which was responsible for three missile sites February 1, 1961 to March 15, 1965:

- 851-A, two miles east-southeast of Lincoln, California
- 851-B, four miles north-northeast of Sutter Buttes, California
- 851-C, six miles north of Chico, California[1]

The squadron's nine HGM-25A Titan 1 intercontinental ballistic missiles were deployed in a 3 x 3 configuration, meaning three missiles at each of the three sites.[2]

Northern California was selected for the location of Titan 1 missile facilities because its geographic area allowed access to secluded regions crucial to avoidance of unwanted attention and publicity regarding large missiles. The three missile complexes were all within 57 miles of Beale Air Force Base, that being the distance to the Chico site. The Lincoln site lay 17 miles from the base, and that in the Sutter Buttes, the one most remote from civilization, 45 miles distant.[3]

Often referred to as the world's smallest mountain range, the Sutter Buttes are a unique volcanic formation consisting of a small circular complex of eroded volcanic lava domes. The highest point, South Butte, reaches an elevation of 2,122 feet.

Photo 3-1

Sutter Buttes, the world's smallest mountain range.
Brian C. Stanford

CONSTRUCTION OF THE SITES

In 1959, the U.S. government took 275 acres of land north of the Chico Municipal Airport from Nathan H. and Harold V. Thomason through eminent domain. Work on the complexes began on January 22, 1960 with the excavation of more than 600,000 cubic yards of earth. The enormous missile facilities at each site were 1,600 feet long, 900 feet wide, and 165 feet underground. Construction of each cost $30 million and included 32,000 cubic yards of concrete, 300 tons of piping, 90 miles of cables and 1,800 separate supply items. The first Titan 1 missile was moved to the Lincoln complex on February 28, 1962, and the last was placed in the Chico complex on April 20, 1962.[4]

Photo 3-2

A Titan I missile emerges from its silo at the Vandenberg Operational System Test Facility in 1960.
US Air Force photograph

DESTRUCTION OF A MISSILE AT CHICO COMPLEX

On May 24, 1962, an explosion destroyed a Titan 1 missile and caused extensive damage to its silo at the Chico complex at 3485 Keefer Road, north of the Chico Municipal Airport.[5]

During the early morning, Joe Herrington, a safety engineer, had been performing atmospheric tests in the missile silos during a fuel and unfuel procedure. In silo No. 1, the tests showed abnormally high liquid oxygen levels, which Herrington had also found in preceding days and reported to his superiors.[6]

A newspaper clipping from 1962 described ensuing events:

> When they finally went down to the bottom of the silo, they discovered that ice had begun to form all around the base of the missile from a valve not properly closing. Herrington's supervisor reportedly kicked the ice at the base of the missile and watched it shatter on the floor.
>
> They began ascending the six flights of stairs to the top of the silo when they came across a white, misty cloud seeping out of one of the liquid oxygen lines connected to the missile. The two rushed up the remaining stairs to warn the rest of the facility as dark, thick smoke began pluming out of silo No. 1.
>
> Herrington hastened his attempts at evacuating base personnel into a single, large elevator that led to the surface. After he squeezed everyone into the elevator, there wasn't any room left for him. So he ran up the auxiliary stairwell assisted by a failing breathing mask, inhaling the black smoke the rest of the way to safety.
>
> At 7:08 a.m., just after everyone got safely to the surface, the missile exploded, destroying the silo and sending large fragments of metal and rock skyward, with chunks and bits of debris raining on the countryside as far as a quarter-mile away. The two silo doors, each weighing 116 tons, were flung open like saloon doors. The silo itself channeled the explosive force straight into the air, acting like an underground cannon.[7]

There were over a hundred men working on that shift. Fortunately, no one died from the explosion, but nearly 60 men were treated at Enloe Hospital for minor injuries and smoke inhalation.[8]

The missile still stood straight in the hole, and its undetonated warhead intact. Not surprising, the explosion at the missile complex was quite a shock for Chico, and it scared a lot of people.[9]

An Air Force investigation concluded that an oxygen valve had stuck open and a blocked vent caused the gas to build up until a spark ignited it. This potential public relations catastrophe received scant attention in the national news because that same day, Scott Carpenter (in the spacecraft *Aurora 7*) was launched into space at Cape Canaveral, Florida, on the Mercury-Atlas 7 mission.[10]

Photo 3-3

Scott Carpenter being assisted into his *Aurora 7* spacecraft for the Mercury Atlas 7 mission on May 24, 1962.
NASA photograph

The Chico complex became operational on March 9, 1963, after the completion of repairs of the extensive blast damage to the silo, at a cost of at least $1,250,000.[11]

DEACTIVATION OF THE THREE COMPLEXES

A year later on May 16, 1964, Defense Secretary Robert McNamara directed the accelerated phase-out of the Titan 1. The first Titan at Chico was taken off alert status on January 4, 1965; the program at the three complexes officially ended eleven weeks later on March 25, 1965.[12]

PROTESTS OF THE CHICO MISSILE COMPLEX

During operation of the missile complex, Chico resident Wilhelmina Taggart made weekly visits to the site to pray for peace. She was soon joined by Florence McLane, and Helen Kinnee. After the silos were closed, the ladies began holding their peace vigil at the corner of Third and Main streets. These protests were the roots of the Chico Peace Endeavor, whose members continue to meet at this corner from 12:30 to 1:30 p.m. every Saturday. Their motto is "We Vigil to End War and Violence."[13]

1962 STATE CHAMPION DOUG PARKER

Photo 3-4

Doug Parker (26) pictured in a portion of the Varsity Basketball Team photograph. Chico High School yearbook *Caduceus '61*

On the heels of Nelson Briles came another great Chico High School athlete, Doug Parker, just one year behind Briles in school. Sports competitions were a unifying, central piece of high school life in the 1960s, and remains so today, particularly in rural areas of America. Parker, a junior when Briles and I were seniors, excelled on the gridiron, basketball court, and track. At track season's end in 1961, he won the North Section Championships quarter mile with a time of 50.0 seconds.

A year later, in early June 1962 (nine days after the explosion of the Titan I missile at the Chico complex), Parker was the State half-mile champion at the California Track & Field Championships. His time of 1:52.2 remains the Chico High school record 64 years later. For decades, track athletes at Chico High have looked up at his superlative time on the record board in the gym and wondered about Doug Parker. His remarkable story is told in the next chapter.

4

1962 State Champion Doug Parker

I've never seen, in 64 years of coaching track, anyone even running the 880 and the hurdles.

—Chuck Sheley (*Chico Enterprise-Record*, Chico State, and Chico High Athletic Hall of Fame member) commenting on Parker's abilities after reviewing draft material for this chapter. Sheley ran 19.2 for the 180-yard low hurdles in 1956, his senior year at Chico High.[1]

Photo 4-1

Front cover of the 1962 California State Track and Field Championships Program.

On Saturday, June 2, 1962, the California State High School Track & Field Championships were held at Modesto Junior College, located in Modesto, a city in California's central valley. When it came time to contest the first of two sections of the 880-yard run, the competitors were called to the starting line of the dirt track. At the crack of the starter's pistol, Chico High's Doug Parker burst off the line. Two laps later he blazed across the finish line in first place, a State Champion. His time of 1:52.2 was a personal best.

Race Results

Place	Name	High School	Section	Time
1	Doug Parker	Chico	North	1:52.2
2	John Garrison	Hoover	San Diego	1:52.7
3	Dennis Breckow	Muir	Southern	1:53.2
4	Bob Blanchard	Hoover	Southern	1:53.5
5	Dave Dunning	Orinda	North Coast	1:53.5
6	Willie Green	Encinal	North Coast	1:54.0

INTERESTING ASIDE

In 1962, they did not have trials for the 880, contestants were split into a two-section final and their times merged for the final standings. Going into the meet, Jonathan Peck (Harvard High School in North Hollywood) was the state leader in the 880 with a 1:53.1 clocking. Peck was the son of movie actor Gregory Peck who traveled north from Hollywood to watch his son run in the state high school championships at Modesto. Peck finished fifth in the first section (won by Parker) and his time did not place him among medal winners. (Gregory Peck, a true track fan, stayed for the whole meet.)

A newspaper article titled "EC's Booth Scores Area's Only Point" describes Parker easily beating Peck:

Photo 4-2

Jonathan Peck, Harvard High School. 1962 California State Track and Field Championships Program

"Powerful Doug Parker of Chico, a 6-3, 187-pound senior, routed touted Jonathan Peck of North Hollywood's Harvard High with a 1:52.2 half. Peck was a badly beaten fifth in 1:55.4 in the first heat with Parker, despite coming in with the best time in the State: 1:53.1"

THE NORTH SECTION

For high school athletic competition, the State of California is divided into the ten sub-divisions, termed Sections, which are identified below.

Map 4-1

California's CIF Sections.

Chico High School is in the Northern Section (commonly called the North Section), which begins to the north-northwest of Sacramento, and extends to the Oregon border minus the North Coast Section.

One measure of how good Parker's effort was (other than that he won the State Meet), is that he still holds the Chico High School record for the half-mile sixty-four years later. Another is that his North Section record was not surpassed until last year (2025) by Jackson Hein.

Hein, from Pleasant Valley High School (Chico High's crosstown rival) ran 1:50.87 for the 800-meter race in winning his heat at the 2025 California State Meet. He ran 1:51.67 to place 4th in the finals the next day. Hein now attends and competes for UC Berkeley (Cal).[2]

Up until 1978, California preps ran the half mile (880), mile, and 2-mile at track meets. On adoption of the metric system, 800m, 1600m, and 3200m races replaced the previous distances. Parker's 1:52.2 880 yards effort converts to a 1:51.5 800 meters. Currently—and perhaps for years to come—two track stars from the Chico community, Hein and Parker, own the top two times ever run for the "two-lapper" in the North Section.[3]

PARKER AN EXCEPTIONAL AND UNIQUE ATHLETE

Doug Parker transferred from Paradise High to Chico High his sophmore year. The mountain community of Paradise is located less than 20 miles up the ridge from Chico. While at Chico High, he lettered in football, basketball, and track & field.

Parker's great talent as a runner was immediately obvious to coaches, teammates and competitors. He validated their great belief in him with one victory at the 1961 North Section Track & Field championships meet, and two the following year. Former track athletes reading this (having already learned that he was State champion in the half-mile in 1962) may be thinking about his 1962 North Section victories, "Okay, he probably won the quarter mile and half mile, or half mile and mile at these championships." If so, they would be wrong.

As a junior in 1961, Parker won the varsity 440-yard run in a time of 50.0 and finished second in the 180-yard low hurdles. The following year (1962) as a senior, he moved up in distance winning the half-mile in 1:53.8, and the low hurdles in 20.2. Next stop, the State meet and individual honors.

Parker was a three-sport letterman in high school, excelling in football and basketball in addition to track & field. Prior to becoming a State Meet champion in track his senior year, he earned All-League, and All-Northern California honors as an End on the football team, and his considerable basketball skills were later highlighted in the 1962 Chico High School *Caduceus* yearbook:

> Doug Parker, a 6'4" returning letterman, has played exceptionally fine basketball this year. His speed and quickness along with his great rebounding and shooting ability has made him a valuable asset to our team.

PARKER GETS FOOTBALL SCHOLARSHIP TO OSU

Doug Parker enrolled at Oregon State University in autumn 1962 on a football scholarship. The following spring, he ran his best time for the half mile up to that point in his freshman track season on May 2, 1963 at Vancouver, Washington. A newspaper article titled "Rook Thinclads Defeat Clark" described his victory:

> Parker paced through a 54-second first lap by Gary Baker registered a 1:52.3 clocking in the 880 with Baker second in 1:54.1.[4]

The "shorthand" article title meant that Oregon State's rookie track squad bested that of Clark College. "Thinclad" is a moniker for track and field athletes, who compete in light uniforms.

WIN OVER CANADIAN OLYMPIAN SIG OHLEMANN

Two weeks later, Parker upset former U of O track star Sig Ohlemann in the 880 at an All Comers track meet at the University of Oregon's Hayward Field. As reported in a newspaper article on May 3, 1963:

> Doug Parker, California state high school 880 champion last year, hung on Ohlemann's shoulder in the final lap and then kicked ahead in the final 75 yards to win in 1:50.3 to Ohlemann's 1:50.4.
>
> "I just got tired," Ohlemann said later, explaining he has had heavy workouts all week in preparation for summer competition and possibly the California Relays at Modesto next Saturday. "He's a good runner, too" Ohlemann said of Parker. Parker enrolled at Oregon State on a football scholarship but has decided to concentrate only on track.[5]

Sig Ohlemann was a 1962 graduate of the University of Oregon, who in 1960 had represented Canada as a member of its track and field team at the Rome Olympics. Prior to the All Comers race at Hayward Field, Ohlemann had competed in the 1963 Pan American Games, winning the silver medal in the 800 meters with a time of 1.48.63. The games were held 27 April - 4 May at São Paulo, Brazil.[6]

1964 NCAA I TRACK & FIELD CHAMPIONSHIPS

The 1964 NCAA Track and Field Championships were contested from June 18th to 20th at Hayward Field in Eugene, Oregon. Parker, now a sophomore, was seeded into the second of four heats for the 800 meters. The first four finishers in each heat would qualify for the semi-final rounds. He finished second in his round with a time of 1.53.9, and moved on to the semi-finals, but did not make the final.

U.S. OLYMPIC TRIALS 800 METERS SEMIFINALS

A newspaper article dated June 21, 1964 informed readers that a Special 800 Meter Runoff had been held and that the winner qualified for the Olympic Trials semifinals at New York. A separate untitled and undated newspaper clipping informed readers:

> OSU qualified Doug Parker into the July 3-4 Olympic trial semifinals when the sophomore won a special 800 – meter runoff. His time was 1:49.1 the same as Seton Hall's George Germann, second with the same clocking.

The Olympic Trials semi rounds for the 800 meters were held on July 3-4. The fifteen competitors who would be vying for three Olympic team member berths were split into two heats, seven in the first heat, eight in the second. Parker did not qualify out of the first heat, ending his Olympic Team hopes. His finishing time in comparison with the other fourteen athletes placed him twelfth overall of the nation's best half-milers assembled there that day.

POSTSCRIPT

An untitled, undated clipped newspaper article reported in 1965:

> Doug Parker, OSU's fine sophomore half-miler of last year, won't be back this spring … he suffered from mononucleosis all fall and didn't run a step. So he dropped out of school winter term, but plans to return to school.

Doug Parker was inducted into the *Chico Enterprise-Record* Sports Hall of Fame in 2000.

HOT RODDIN'

Photo 4-3

Two examples of hot rods.
PublicDomainPictures.net

I loved cars and particularly hot rods. In the 1960s, hot rods were commonly seen on the streets of Chico, mostly driven by adult males, a majority of them veterans. The hot-rodding culture basically began with veterans returning home after World War II, who were not content with standard jalopies and sedans. Empowered by mechanical skills learned in the military, coupled with a desire for competition, adrenaline, innovation, and entertainment they stripped down and souped up their Detroit mass produced cars.

The next two short chapters are devoted to car culture in Chico, in the 1960s, which included teenagers cruising "the 'Nade," and race track action at the Silver Dollar Speedway.

5

Cruisin' and My First Two Cars

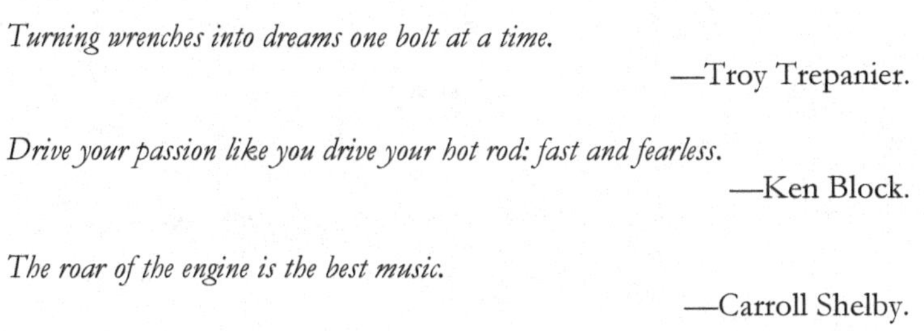

Turning wrenches into dreams one bolt at a time.

—Troy Trepanier.

Drive your passion like you drive your hot rod: fast and fearless.

—Ken Block.

The roar of the engine is the best music.

—Carroll Shelby.

Hot rods, abundant in the 1960s, represented creativity, freedom, and the rebellious spirit found in car culture. Young men such as myself, with limited resources but with a desire to experience a sense of freedom and escape from everyday life, mostly had to settle for cruising in whatever car was available to them. Obtaining a candidate car ideal for being "hot rodded" and doing so was expensive!

As detailed in the following chapter, there were jalopy races (early stock car dirt track racing) in Chico in the 1950s when I was a kid, and in 1962, my first school year at Chico State, sprint car racing was introduced at the speedway which continues to this day.

Of course, there were also car races by high school kids on city streets, including the Esplanade which was termed Cruisin' the 'Nade. Chico High students, including me, "tooled around" which meant that we drove up and down the Esplanade. Honking at girls and honking at friends. Once downtown, the typical route was to start by the college and cruise out to the A&W Drive-in and back. Gas was 25 cents a gallon then. It would be a much bigger commitment now to make those many circuits.

Far from Cruisin' was drag racing "the 'Nade." I remember sitting at a stop light in my parents' 1957, four-door Pontiac. It was so powerful with a big V-8! Or so I thought. Who pulls up beside me in his brand new Corvair Spyder, Doug Timmons. Doug and I were classmates at Chico High. He motioned that he wanted to drag me and I motioned back in the affirmative.

When the light turned green, I hit the gas and took off and looked back to see him in my dust (err, rubber). He was not there. I looked at the right lane way ahead of me and there he was in all his glory. I had not considered the weight of a 1957 4-door Pontiac compared to a little Corvair Spyder with its air-cooled 150-horsepower rear-mounted engine, and a 4-speed stick shift.

Photo 5-1

Models shown clockwise: Corvette Sting Ray Convertible, Corvair Monza Spyder Convertible, Chevrolet Impala Super Sport Convertible, Chevy II Nova 400 Super Sport Convertible. Center: Soap Box Derby Racer, built by All-American boys.
Chico State College *Wildcat*, March 15, 1963

Doug had a passion for automobiles and turned that into a lifelong career with Timmons Automotive Performance, installing big-block Chevy engines in Jaguars (many of them XJ6 sedans). Over several decades, he did 412 Jaguar conversions termed "lumping." Additional information about his business, from an *Enterprise-Record* article titled "Timmons: More than 400 Jaguars in 40 years" (published December 20, 2009) is provided in the next section.[1]

TIMMONS AUTOMOBILE PERFORMANCE

I love speed. I love racing.

—Remark by Doug Timmons, who shared a love of hot-rod racing with local attorney J.D. Zink in the 1960s. Among their race cars was a record-setting A class junior fueler. Junior fuelers engaged in "David vs. Goliath" drag racing with larger dragsters.[2]

Timmons launched his Timmons Automotive Performance business in 1969 after, while studying engineering, he found that tinkering with engines and cars was preferable. Doug quickly built a reputation for producing cars with a creamy ride, varoom under the hood, and the appreciation of an excellent car. He noted about the final product, "there's music in the tailpipe."[3]

In an interview in 2009, Timmons explained the reason behind the then 406 Jaguars he'd rebuilt, "Great cars, lousy engine. They blow out." So he put a Corvette engine under the hood of these cars, and made sure their interiors and exteriors were "cherry"—including burl wood walnut dashes he made by hand.[4]

Timmons worked most frequently with Jaguars because of their driving comfort and safe bodies, but also put a better engine under the hoods of other type cars. Creating performance cars is how he made his living, and his customers ran the gamut from doctors and lawyers to local school teachers. Word of mouth and repeat customers were his strongest allies, and customers, often waiting months for a custom car, were very appreciative.[5]

Sadly, Doug Timmons passed away on April 16, 2024.

MY FIRST TWO CARS

My first car was a 4-door 1953 Chevy, which I purchased in 1962. It was painted "hospital green." There was a stylish visor over the windshield. It had been owned by a little Old Lady from…No not Pasadena, but Chico. Still, it was mine. My dad helped me pick it out from a used car lot, because he thought it would be safe. Mind you, this was not my idea of a car, but it was a car and hence, independence.

Photo 5-2

1953 Chevy 4-door sedan (210 series) similar to mine.

The first thing I did was take it to a body shop and have the visor removed and molded over. Also, to come off was the corny hood ornament. The hood was molded and it was painted blue, but it was still a 4-door and no matter what you did to it, it was still a 4-door. Next, what do you do with old-fashioned hub caps? Well, you remove them and paint your rims black. Then you get fake white-walls. But that's not all, you purchase a set of "spinners." I let my girlfriend take it for a spin and I admired those spinners dispersing a glimpse of sunlight in an agitated fashion.

My next car was a 1950 Olds painted a metallic blue. I got it in 1963, after selling my previous car to my best friend, Bruce Wadlington. I was told it was the second-prettiest car in Chico. Gary Griswold owned the prettiest. It was a two-door 1955 Chevy which was painted a Pearlescent Maroon and had white Naugahyde interior. My Oldsmobile had to be worked on, so of course, since I was an Industrial Arts major at Chico State, I took it to the Auto Shop.

Somebody suggested that the carburetor needed to be cleaned out. So, I dutifully went to the auto parts store and bought carburetor cleaner. Everything was OK until I pulled onto West First Street which went by the front of Chico State College. I looked in my rearview mirror, and to my horror, I could not see anything but white smoke. Students lived in the houses that lined the southside of the street and they were laughing. I had made quite an impression…

6

Silver Dollar Speedway

The smell of fuel and dirt is my favorite scent.

—Tony Stewart.

You can't put a price on the adrenaline that dirt racing brings.

—Jason Baugh.

From 1962 through the present, Friday nights in Chico are marked by the roar of engines of sprint cars racing at the Silver Dollar Speedway. The high-banked, quarter-mile clay oval racetrack is sited on the Silver Dollar Fairgrounds at aptly named Fair Street. Noise from the track is prevalent in Chico, but is masked by city and traffic noises. The auto racing is easily heard in surrounding areas outside of town where it is quieter.

Opened in 1962, the track remains home to Friday night auto racing and currently hosts multiple high-profile events including:

- Annual marquee Gold Cup Race of Champions
- David Tarter Memorial
- Mini Gold Cup, and
- The Fall Nationals in tribute to Stephen Allard[1]

The inaugural Gold Cup Race of Champions was in 1951 with Johnny Soares winning the first trophy. Initially held in Sacramento at Hughes Stadium and later Capital Speedway, the event moved in 1980 to the Silver Dollar Speedway.[2]

David Tarter died at the age of 30 in 2012 when a freak accident in the pit area took his life. He had been a regular participant at the Silver Dollar Speedway and former track rookie of the year.

Stephen Allard, a two-time track champion and winner of 18 career feature event wins at Chico, passed away on December 24, 2012. Since then, the Speedway has hosted the Fall Nationals event in his honor.[3]

LOCAL RACING HISTORY

The Speedway was the fourth auto racing track to be built in the Chico area. The first was a half-mile track, sited approximately where the present track is located. From 1948 to 1950, Big Sprint Car Races were held at this location, with Lennie Low the dominant driver. In 1950, the Chico Auto Racing Association was formed and Jalopy races were contested at the Fairgrounds that year and the next. In 1952 races were held off Highway 32 at a track built around Hann Baseball Field.[4]

Racing moved to the Chico Speedway at the end of East Eight Street in 1953, where racing flourished until 1962. Finally, in 1962 the Valley Auto Racing association was formed and the present track was constructed. From its inception, the Silver Dollar Speedway has been the only track in northern California to operate on a primarily Friday night weekly schedule.[5]

410 SPRINT CARS

Photo 6-1

410 Sprint car race at the Silver Dollar Speedway.
Cali Dirt Video photograph

The "410 sprint car" nomenclature results from a 410 cubic inch engine limit introduced in 1962 by the American Sprint Car Series (USCS). This was done to promote parity among competitors and reduce engine costs. Current engines are based on the Chevrolet small-block V8 engine but feature numerous upgrades made over the years for enhanced performance and durability.[6]

The sprint cars themselves have very high power-to-weight ratios, with weights of approximately 1,400 pounds including the driver, and power outputs of over 900 horsepower. The wings with sideboards increase the downforce generated on the car (lessening the chance of going airborne) and help to turn the car while cornering.[7]

7

Active Navy Duty

I partied too much at Chico State in autumn 1963 and, following a tallying of semester grades, received a letter from the college asking me not to return for a while. Girls, cars, alcohol, and a part-time job, on top of a full academic load, had been my undoing.

When I began my freshman year at Chico State, I was not a hard-core drinker. Then I met Gene Smithson. Hard drinking hot-rodder. I would only drink Vodka and Seven-Up. Gene drank beer. I did not like the taste of beer. So parties at his place were different mixtures of libations. I grew to like beer and that made parties easier.

Gene lived in a rental on Rio Chico Way, across Warner Street on the southside of Big Chico Creek, near the Chico State Engineering Building. Or let's say the basement of a two-story Victorian house. A basement where many a party took place. Who had time for school? We formed a drinking club and were in the process of acquiring a 1948, gold, DeSoto convertible for our club car. There were various characters in "The Club." First was Al Von Bargen who could take a 16-ounce can of beer and chug it in milliseconds. Then there was Gene who could polish off a case of beer before passing out. Finally, I was designated the mascot; I could drink less and get drunkest the fastest.

Having received the news that I had "flunked out" of Chico State, and not wanting to commute the hundred-mile-round-trip each day to attend the nearest junior college fifty miles south in Yuba City, I decided to go on active duty in the Navy. I had joined the Naval Reserve in September 1961, following high school graduation, and as a part of my six-year enlistment I had an obligation to serve two years on active duty. From March 1, 1964 till January 23, 1967, I was a sailor in Uncle Sam's Navy.[1]

ABDUCTED ON EVE OF DEPARTURE

Since I had signed up with the Navy and I had flunked out of Chico State, my time to go active was the next day. Unbeknownst to me, my friends had been planning a surprise going-away party for me. I spent my last day with a couple of my friends out looking for the KHSL (pronounce Kahissle) Bug, a contest sponsored by a local radio station. After not finding it, I headed home to clean up for my date that night with my girlfriend. Having my friends still with me, they suggested that we drive up the Esplanade to find Al Von Bargen, another friend. As we passed by the Sno-White Drive-in, they said they saw Al behind Sno-Whites. They suggested I pull around to say HI. I protested that I had to go home and get ready for my date.

However, I turned and drove to the rear of the drive-in, where a number of hoodlums (actually my friends) pulled me out of my car, tied me up and blindfolded me. They told me that we were driving to Nevada to a brothel and they would pay for me to have a (for a better word) great experience.

I protested that I must meet my girlfriend for our date, when in reality I was excited about this great adventure. They said that the next thing I would see would be a naked woman.

We drove around for quite some time. I was told we were going to Los Molinos to pick up another guy. We eventually stopped, and I was carried up into a building bound and blindfolded. I was placed in the center of the living room floor and my hands were untied. I lifted off my blindfold and there were all of my friends and my girlfriend. I was later told that I had surprise and hurt on my face. It seemed that everyone in attendance knew what I was expecting.

There was a keg of beer and a bunch of us guys got hammered. We stood up and sang "She Loves You" by the Beatles. Even though my hair was short, I managed to pull some of it down my forehead—just like the Beatles.

STUDENT AT NAVAL STATION, TREASURE ISLAND

Photo 7-1

Oversized panoramic of Naval Training Station Treasure Island, CA, circa 1918-1920. Naval History and Heritage Command photograph #UA 571.59

While a student at "TI" (Naval Training Station, Treasure Island, in the San Francisco Bay), I had a college buddy (introduced at the top of this chapter) who lived in nearby Richmond, California. Gene Smithson and I had met at Chico State in the Fall semester of 1961 while taking industrial arts classes, and we both really liked fast cars and women. I had decided to buy Gene's '56 Chevy, and one Friday night we were working feverishly in his garage to get the car ready for me to test drive it home to Chico. We finished "wrenching" about midnight.[2]

This beauty—which had more problems than were evident to me—was "cherry" with a bored-out Corvette V-8 engine and a four-speed stick; for a young man of that era, cars just didn't get any better than that. It was metallic green with orange "nerf bars," metal devices which replaced the front bumper. The theory was that since nerf bars were much lighter than bumpers, their use increased the car's power-to-weight ratio, making it faster. The racer (our term for a hot rod) had four-inch headers that connected to dump tubes behind the front wheels—which gave the hot rod a menacing look—and exhaust pipes that led aft. The car was everything I dreamed of, in stark contrast to the 1956 four-door, 6-cylinder Chevy, with the shifter on the column, that I owned.[3]

Photo 7-2

My '56 Chevy did not have the necessary pedigree to be turned into a hotrod; it was a lowly four-door family car, versus a two-door "screaming machine."

Gene's brother, Larry, and his buddy were planning on going to Alaska with four dollars between them and wanted a ride north. Both had been rejected by the Marines. Apparently despite the tattoos of eagles they had acquired on their chests, other factors had failed to impress the Marine recruiters—likely a lack of good judgement. We rolled out of Richmond, on the San Francisco Bay, around midnight, and headed for Chico, 180 miles to the north-northeast. By the time we reached Williams, a little farming town approximately one hundred miles up the road, the linkage for the first and reverse gears had gone out.[4]

I pulled into a Chevron station for repairs. As I exited the well-lit station, I did not realize that I had failed to turn my headlights on. The car's engine was roaring because "jury rigged" header gaskets (pieces of tin foil that Gene had installed) had blown out on the highway. Leaving the station, the fire-breathing hot rod sounded like an F-4 fighter aircraft preparing to take off. The engine had a three-quarter race camshaft—which allowed greater quantities of gas and air to enter the combustion chambers, producing more power and noise—and a muffler rendered ineffective by exhaust leaks from the header dump tube.[5]

ENCOUNTER WITH THE LAW

I fought the law and the law won.

—Lyrics from the song "I Fought the Law" by Bobby Fuller.

Well, they arrested me and put me in jail
And called my pop to throw my bail
He said, "Son, you're gonna drive me to drinking
If you don't quit driving that Hot Rod Lincoln"

—The 1955 song "Hot Rod Lincoln" by Charlie Ryan is a rockabilly classic about a highspeed race between a Ford Model A and a Cadillac. An encounter I had with the law did not involve racing, and I was not thrown in jail. But I, too, incurred the wrath of my father, and my actions resulted in a painful "lightening" of my meager wallet.

As I was waiting at an intersection for the traffic light to change, I noticed a police officer to my left across the intersection, writing a ticket for a car he had pulled over. He noticed me and motioned with his flashlight for me to pull over as well. As I started to comply with this order, one of my two passengers said, "You can get away from him!" I don't know why I listened to a guy the Marines had rejected, but I did. After the light turned, I drove one block, turned left, then left again, then pulled over and turned off the engine. We were then one block west of our original position. We could see the police officer searching for us on perpendicular streets to the north and south. Fortunately, he never came down the street we were on.[6]

After a while I crept out of town. When we got to Colusa, an even smaller farm town farther north, a sheriff pulled us over. I asked him what I had done, because I was going the speed limit. He replied, "There's a man from Williams who wants to see you!" I got as pale as a ghost and felt sick to my stomach. Within a short time, the Williams police officer I thought I had successfully evaded arrived and jumped out of his cruiser. I handed him my Navy ID card and he said, "You know Mike, I was in the Navy, the most I would have given you was a $12.00 ticket, but now I am going to get you for $300.00 if I get you for a penny."[7]

He wrote me up for speeding, reckless driving, driving without lights, and eluding a police vehicle. I had not been speeding nor driving recklessly, but that didn't matter. Due to my poor judgment, I had to pay a large fine, leaving me insufficient money to buy Gene's car. After arriving in Chico, I also had to tell my father what had transpired. He took a day off from work, and travelled to the Williams courthouse for my hearing. Because he vouched for my good character, the judge lowered the fine from $300.00 to $200.00. This helped some, but still left me short of the "scratch" necessary to buy my dream car, leaving me with my "heap" and not Gene's cherry ride.[8]

Problems with cars, and also girls and alcohol, would continue to haunt me. As discussed later, most of the problems with cars resulted from me spending all my spare time drinking and pursuing girls instead of doing maintenance on my cars. For readers much younger than I, who today own reliable cars, the automobiles of the 1950s required much work to keep them on the road. One Friday afternoon I left for Chico, and made it just past Fairfield when suddenly my ride developed a shaking that made me think that the engine was going to tear loose from the motor mounts. I had to pull over and have my car towed to a holding yard until I could figure out what to do about it. I then hitchhiked to Chico, because I had a date the following night with my girlfriend. She was a beauty and I did not want to disappoint her and, in the process, really disappoint me![9]

STARLITE DRIVE-IN THEATER

Saturday night found the two of us in my parents' car, parked in the back row of the Starlite Drive–in Theater. We were engaged in a tangled and heated display of affection, when all of a sudden there was a rapping on the driver-side window. I looked up at a man who I immediately recognized as her father. Was he going to pull me out of the car and thrash me within an inch of my life? He had always been so cool, and he liked me. (The way things had been progressing with his daughter, it's a good thing that he didn't show up ten minutes later).[10]

"The first drive-in Motion Picture Theater popped up in 1938. When the Starlite Drive-In (holding more people and autos than one might expect) came into existence in 1948 it was the only drive-in north of Sacramento and south of Washington State. The Starlite is quite an antique compared to modern drive-ins. With just one screen, a snack bar and an old-fashioned film projector pit area right in the middle of the theater lot, one thinks of being thrown back to another era." (CSU Chico *Orion*, April 21, 1982)

I rolled down the window and meekly said, "Hi." Mr. B. was some kind of a special guy. My girlfriend must have told him about my dilemma with my car, prompting him to come to the drive-in. He smiled and asked for the keys to my Chevy, as a prelude to going to Fairfield to rescue my car. He brought it back to Chico for me and parked it in front of my parents' house.[11]

As indicated in the quoted material on the preceding page from an article, "Chico's great American drive-in theater" published in the California State University, Chico *Orion*, April 21, 1982, the Starlite was built in 1948. It offered enjoyable summer entertainment and, like drive-ins across the United States, was a popular "make-out spot." During the part of the year when the Starlite was closed, owing to cold/rainy weather, there remained the indoor Senator and El Rey theaters downtown. The preceding photograph and ads (in clockwise order) are from the *Orion*, April 21, 1982; *Wildcat*, December 3, 1967; and *Wildcat*, May 12, 1967.[12]

My car needed a lot of work, and I was not going to give up precious liberty time that could be spent drinking and dating to work on it. I offered to sell my car to Mr. B for one hundred dollars, thinking that he might want to fix it up for his daughter, who did not have a car at the time. He declined. He likely also did not want to devote all his time to working on it, and besides, the engine was probably blown. So, the car remained parked in front of my parents' house. My dad eventually told me later, on another weekend liberty, that we should at least look under the hood. He opened the hood and removed the valve cover, and immediately discovered the obvious problem. A retainer holding the valve spring in place had sheared off allowing the valve to drop down and cause all of the problems.[13]

JACK'S AUTO WRECKING

Dad and I went down to the local junk yard, Jack's Auto Wrecking at 2240 Park Avenue, with the retainer in hand. Jack had previously helped me many times with used parts for the '53 Chevy and '50 Olds coupe I had previously owned. Back then, working on your car was a weekly chore. We showed him the retainer and asked if he had something like it. He scuffed his boot through the gravel on the ground and picked up an exact duplicate of what we needed. We asked him how much, and with a grin he said, "Nothing." Now that's customer service. We returned home. Dad took the valve spring and put it in his bench vice. He cranked it down and twisted a piece of wire to hold the spring compressed. We took the spring and the retainer out to the car. After installing it, Dad snipped the wire and the spring sprang into place. I left the car in Chico and eventually sold it. It was spotted around Chico for years, and may still be running today.[14]

ORDERS TO A SHIP

Returning to Treasure Island and finishing school there, I received orders to the destroyer USS *Hopewell* (DD-681), homeported in San

Diego, California. (My attendance at the school had added a one-year extension of my two-year active-duty obligation.) I reported aboard *Hopewell* in June 1964. Her schedule when not on deployment and back in homeport was like that of other Navy ships: periodic under way periods for training and exercises to gain and maintain warfare proficiency, interspersed with occasional visits to liberty ports for crew rest and recreation. Very rigorous training and certification of all warfare areas was the order of the day prior to departure of a ship on a deployment. For *Hopewell* and other U.S. West Coast-based ships at that time, this meant a six-month "WestPac" (deployment to the Western Pacific), and soon thereafter duty on the gunline off Vietnam.

Photo 7-3

Destroyer USS *Hopewell* (DD-681) at sea during the 1960s.
Naval History and Heritage Command photograph #NH 89658-KN

CHICO HIGH SCHOOL FOOTBALL

Autumn Friday nights in Chico found large numbers of high school students in the bleachers for home football games, whether they were true fans raptly watching the action on the field, or were there to enjoy the social atmosphere. During my first year aboard the *Hopewell*, there was an exciting running back at Chico High School. The next chapter is devoted to Charles "Charlie" Crabtree, a high school All-Northern California football player, and perhaps the finest running back to ever play for the Red & Gold.

8

Chico High's 1963 Football Team

Charlie wasn't a sprinter, not out of the blocks. Running backs come with different talents, different running styles. Charlie had sufficient speed, and good dodging skills, but he was exceptional at bouncing off tackles and when wrapped up, churning on, often carrying a defender a few yards. Modest-sized Charlie didn't have blazing speed, but great agility in running the ball, and was extremely tough. His overall athleticism was truly remarkable.

—Tim O'Neill, Chico High teammate of Charlie Crabtree, who was a year junior to him and also a running back.[1]

Charlie was one quiet tough cookie. An exceptional football player who along with Gary Houser was recruited by Tommy Prothro to play for the Oregon State Beavers. He returned after sophomore year to marry his high school sweetheart and did not return to Corvallis. Under [Chico High track coach] Mel Jones' watchful eye Charlie and I trained together during afterschool workouts. Mel added a morning workout; Charlie would pick me up 6:00 and drive to Bidwell golf course and run "tee to green" jingle jog to next tee box and build up to green. When we finished a stop for milk and donuts…shower at school. Oh, so many wonderful memories and I could never beat him.

—Sam Simmons, Chico High teammate of Charlie Crabtree on the the football and track teams. Simmons was the quarterback and played safety on defense. He ran the half mile and was on the mile relay team in track. During winter sports, Simmons lettered in basketball and Crabtree in wrestling.[2]

"Rock" McClellan and "Blackie" Gilbert coached Chico High's 1963 football team as they had in previous years and ensuing ones. (1963-64 School Year team, which played in autumn 1963.) Chico High male coaches during this era were pretty much from the same mold. Outstanding high school athletes from Chico or nearby towns, who served in the military in World War II or in the Korean War—some saw combat action.

Photo 8-1

L-R: Coaches "Rock" McClellan and "Blackie" Gilbert.
Chico High School yearbook *Caduceus '61*

Joseph "Rock" McClellan graduated from Red Bluff High School in 1939, attended college, then enlisted in the Navy in 1941. He served with the "Seabees" (Naval construction battalion) on Guadalcanal and Espiritu Santo in the Solomon Islands. Clifford "Blackie" Gilbert was the 1939 Chico High School Student Body president and then began Chico State that fall. He joined the U.S. Marine Corps in 1941, and was attached to the Joint Assault Signal Corps in the South Pacific. Following the atomic bombing of Nagasaki, "Blackie" and eleven other Marines were the first US troops taken into the highly radiated area to serve as reconnaissance drivers.[3]

Track coach (Melvin Richard) Mel Jones, cited in the quoted material, served as a radarman aboard the amphibious attack transport USS *Mellette* (APA-156) in World War II, and earned the Purple Heart Medal for being wounded in combat. Jones participated in baseball, track, and boxing at Chico State, becoming a Far Western Conference boxing champion in 1950. Mel passed away on September 3, 2019, at age 94, greatly beloved in the Chico community.

Following their discharge, McClellan, Gilbert, Jones, and others of their ilk, attended Chico State on the GI Bill, participated in sports and were All-Conference athletes. Upon finishing their education, they accepted teaching/coaching positions at Chico High School.

The demeanor and presence of this type men demanded respect and they got it. Young men in their classrooms or on their athletic fields knew without being told, to listen when they were talking, and to apply themselves to the task at hand. If someone was doing something they shouldn't, they received "direct feedback." Teachers and coaches were not required to receive sensitivity training back then.

The same atmosphere existed in shop classes taught by veterans. Clarence Pentico (a Chico State Athletic Hall of Fame football player), was the woodshop teacher at Chico Junior High. On the first day of class, he would pick up a 3-inch 10-penny nail and drive it through a pine board by repeatedly striking the head of the metal spike with the callused heel of his hand. This non-verbal demonstration sent a clear message to freshman boys regarding who was in charge.

1963 FOOTBALL SEASON

Like a political rally, a locker room emits the mood of the team, cool with anticipation of thumping a weak opponent or fearful and tense against a peer competitor. Individually, every player is aware he will be tested and is justifiably anxious. My coaches were all business. They dampened outbursts, raised moods, huddled with key players. After the game, in the bus or locker room, emotions were just as tense but in a celebratory or depressed way depending on the outcome. Before a game, there was so much testosterone boiling you could smell it. On the turf you quivered with anticipation, muscles tense, eyes scanning the field, the stands, the coach and the game -- all melting into the roar of the crowd, and if it was you that made that touchdown, it was all the more exhilarating.

—Tim O'Neill describing team atmosphere immediately prior to and following a football game, and exhilaration during it.[4]

Chico High's 1963 football team achieved modest success, finishing with a 4-4-1 season record. On that team were two stars, Fullback and End Gary Houser and Halfback Charlie Crabtree. Among the finest players to ever lace up football cleats at Chico High, they also excelled at other sports. In the previous school year, Houser had been recipient of the Maddy Madsen award for football, and was chosen as a member of the All-Northern Athletic League basketball team.

This year, Crabtree was All-Northern California, All-North, All League (Northern) and Player of the Year. Over the football season, he netted 573 yards on 131 carries for a 4.4 average; scored 13 touchdowns and two conversions; and caught 30 passes. (Additional information about Charles' laurels is provided in a press release in the following section.) Charlie also received local Maddy Madsen and Max Lee awards, and was the North Section half-mile champion in track.

In the intervening winter sports season, Houser once again played varsity basketball, while Crabtree competed at the 154-pound weight class for the wrestling team.

NORTH-SOUTH SHRINE GAME

Photo 8-2

Charlie Crabtree senior portrait, and North-South Shrine Game Press Book. Charlie was identified in the press book as "Chuck," and also later in football statistics while a running back at Oregon State University.
Chico High School yearbook *Caduceus* '64

The North-South Shrine Game was a prestigious annual postseason high school football all-star game that took place from 1948 to 1973, with a final appearance in 1976. The game was sponsored by Shriners International, with proceeds used to support the Shriners Hospitals for Crippled Children. The event featured top high school seniors from northern California playing against the top seniors from southern California, often in the Los Angeles Coliseum. Starting players in these games included future NFL stars and college football legends, making the Shrine Game a significant event in high school football history.

The 1964 North-South Shrine Game was played on Thursday, July 30th, which is interesting as High School Class of 1964 players had already graduated. It appears that the scheduling of the game was meant to allow great preps "one more day in the sun," and to fuel excitement among football fans prior to the impending fall season.

The North's 25-man team roster is shown below, followed by that of the South Team. Both are from the Press Book for the game.

North Team Roster

Player	Address
Abascal, Manuel	700 Maud Ave., San Leandro
Abono, Cecil	237 Calistoga Dr., Pittsburg
Becknell, John	1915 N. Funston Ave., Stockton
Bittner, Bob	15 N. Orange, Lodi
Brill, Marty	1870 University Ave., Palo Alto
Calcagno, Ray	617 Brunswick, San Francisco
Chaney, Jim	248 Nancy Lane, Pleasant Hill
Crabtree, Chuck	Rt. 3, Box 261 River Rd., Chico
Deschler, John	361 Texas, San Francisco
Flores, Dan	1621 E. Eighth St., Stockton
Grissom, Lowell	Lathrop Rd., Lathrop
Hackler, John	12878 E. Kings Canyon, Sanger
Hildreth, Omri	37 Stringtown, Weed
Reames, Vern	288 N. Oak View, Farmersville
Rossovich, Tim	2310 California St., Mountain View
Schomaker, Mike	2800 Westgate, Concord
Shea, Terry	1017 Westwood Dr., San Jose
Sherman, Jim	3929 Dry Creek Rd., Sacramento
Simmons, Cliff	581 Ridgeway, Yuba City
Stahl, John	1153 "R" St., Fresno
Staley, Bill	2617 Cherry Lane, Walnut Creek
Stanley, Steve	326 Channing Way, Exeter
Swanson, Dave	835 W. Iris, Visalia
Van Lengen, Jerry	7073 21st St., Sacramento
Winstead, Greg	555 Oak St., Mountain View

South Team Roster

Player	Address
Adamo, Marv	7031 Texhoma Ave., Van Nuys
Allen, Ralph	899 N. Madison, Pasadena
Bassler, Rich	1833 Seventh St., Apt. 6, Santa Monica
Curtis, Mike	1934 Chariton St., Los Angeles
Drake, Ron	9606 Lochinvar, Pico Rivera
Erquiaga, John	3774 Armstrong, San Diego
Heckman, Bob	1356 Quincy, Long Beach
Hokanson, Vic	7792 13th St., Westminster
Kelley, Carlton	1166 W. 38th Pl., Los Angeles
Key, Randy	2544 13th Ave., Los Angeles
Kraus, Steve	389 Lexington Ave., Goleta
Lowe, Obia	1710 Victoria Ave., Los Angeles
McCullough, Earl	1915 Lewis Ave., Long Beach
Mercado, Hank	1331 Stillman Ave., Redlands
Motley, Marv	2108 Orange, Long Beach
O'Malley, Jack	1742 Neptune Ave., Wilmington
Page, Toby	10112 Cowan Heights Dr., Santa Ana
Parks, Ted	519 E. 20th St., Santa Ana
Pritchett, Ron	1944 Elsereno Ave., Pasadena
Rios, Dennis	12203 Sunnybrook Lane, Whittier
Scarpace, Mike	7231 Amestoy, Van Nuys
Smith, Art	516 S. 45th St., San Diego
Swanson, Steve	6773 Citronell Ave., Pico Rivera
Swartz, Don	8049 Dunfield Ave., Los Angeles
Young, Adrian	15142 Badlona Dr., La Mirada

Included in the Press Book was the height and weight of each player and the record of their high school team the previous season. The book also offered press members the average weight of each team's line, backs, and overall team.

Chuck Crabtree H 6-0 170 Chico, 4-4-1

North Team	South Team
Line average: 217 lbs.	Line average: 211 lbs.
Back average: 192 lbs.	Back average: 183 lbs.
Team average: 207 lbs.	Team average: 200 lbs.

On the whole, North players were a little larger than those of the South, but Crabtree was one of the lighter running backs.

SOUTH "BLOWOUT" OF THE NORTH

The South crushed the North that day, scoring at will and winning the game 41-0. The Press Book, provided to correspondents after the game, summarized the lopsided action:

> A defense which set up the most explosive offense in Shrine game history—five touchdowns and a safety—was hailed as the main reason behind the South's 41-0 thrashing of the North, before a crowd of 45,527 on July 30, 1964.
>
> The Southerners, individually and collectively, broke 10 game records and tied three others in scoring the most one-sided victory in the 13 years of the series….
>
> In totaling 20 of 29 passes the South was able to total 407 yards on offense.

Among the players on the powerful South Team were quarterback Toby Page and halfback Earl McCullouch (surname misspelled McCullough in the South roster). Three years later, Page would quarterback the USC Trojans' 1967 national championship team. He played a key role in its 21-20 victory over UCLA by calling the famous "23-Blast" audible which set up O.J. Simpson's game-breaking 64-yard touchdown run in the fourth quarter.

Earl McCullouch also played college football for the USC Trojans and was selected by the Detroit Lions of the National Football League in the first round of the 1968 NFL draft. McCullouch played seven seasons for the Lions and Saints. He had 124 catches for 2,319 yards and scored 19 touchdowns. McCullouch was the world record holder for the 110 meters high hurdles July 1967 to July 1969. He ran the start leg on USC's 4×110-yard relay team that set the world record in 1967.

Each of the North's players were high school football stars at their schools, in their leagues, and larger areas of the north state. They had the misfortune in that game of being matched up against future Division I University stars—one with world-class speed. In winning the game 41-0, the South team's offense gained a total of 271 yards passing and 136 yards rushing. In comparison, the North produced a miniscule 56 net yards passing and negative 30 yards rushing.

Charlie Crabtree had the second highest production among seven North players who carried the ball over the course of the game. He touched the ball four times, gaining a total of 14 yards, an average of 3.5 yards per carry. Cliff Simmons (Yuba City High School) was the top running back for the North, gaining 19 yards, 2.7 per carry.

The player sketch devoted to Crabtree in the Press Book informed correspondents of his offensive output during the 1963 football season, and of other interests, hunting and fishing, and playing the guitar.

CHARLES (CHUCK) SCOTT CRABTREE, Chico, 6-0, 170: All-Northern California, All-North, All-League (Northern) and Player of the Year ... Voted team's Most Valuable Player ... Netted 573 yards on 131 carries for a 4.4 average ... Scored 13 touchdowns and two conversions ... Caught 30 passes ... Halfback on defense ... Team captain ... Above average student ... Preparing for engineering career ... Likes to hunt and fish ... Plays guitar ... Also participates in track (880 and 440) and wrestling ... Probably will enroll at Oregon State ... Born in Chico, Calif., Aug. 9, 1946.

GREATNESS CREATES A BECKONING LIGHT

College coaches scout high school talent, assessing future potential of outstanding prep athletes for success in their programs. Tommy Prothro (James Thompson Prothro Jr.), head coach at Oregon State University from 1955 to 1964, recruited Gary Houser and Charlie Crabtree to play football for the Beavers. Houser and Crabtree followed Doug Parker to OSU, who Prothro had enrolled on a football scholarship in 1962. (Prothro moved to the professional ranks of the National Football League in 1971 as head coach of the Los Angeles Rams for two seasons, then the San Diego Chargers from 1974 to 1978.)

Gary Houser's great success at Oregon State is taken up in a later chapter, titled "A Change of Traditional Rivals." Chuck Crabtree was a running back for the OSU varsity team in 1965.

1965 Oregon State University Running Back Production

Name	Attempts	Total Yards	Average
Pete Pifer	234	1095	4.7
Bob Grim	87	398	4.6
Fred Schweer	41	138	3.4
Chuck Crabtree	13	80	6.2
Charlie Shaw	14	59	4.2
Cliff Watkins	9	46	5.1
Clayton Calhoun[5]	3	3	1.0

Pete Pifer, the team's workhorse and leading running back, rushed for 1,095 yards and six touchdowns, an Oregon State single-season record. Not surprisingly, Crabtree didn't play much, but did average 6.2 yards per carry when he had the opportunity to run the ball. Pifer was drafted by the New York Giants in the 11th round of the 1967 NFL Draft. He played that season for the Westchester Bulls, a minor league American football team based in Mount Vernon, New York, and part of the Atlantic Coast Football League.[6]

1964 NORTH SECTION HALF-MILE CHAMPION

Returning to the subject of Crabtree's unique athleticism while at Chico High School, he was the 1964 North Section champion in the half-mile, winning the race with a time of 1:56.0. Being a middle-distance runner, and not a sprinter as running backs usually are, evidences his reliability on agility and elusiveness on the gridiron. Not possessing great pure speed and being of modest size—he wrestled at 154 pounds (slimmed down from his football playing weight)—Charlie being a running back in the now defunct PAC-8 (Pacific-8 Conference) warrants admiration. These universities comprised UC Berkeley, Stanford, USC, UCLA, Washington, Washington State, Oregon, and Oregon State.

Crabtree and two Chico High track teammates qualified for, but did not have opportunity to compete in the State Championships. As reported in the *Enterprise-Record* (date of article unknown):

> Chico Panther thinclads Mike Borzage, Charlie Crabtree and Don Hall earned the right to participate in the California Interscholastic Federation Track and Field Championships with victories in the hurdles [120HH: 15.2, 180LH: 21.1], 880-yard run [1:56.0] and broad jump [22' 3.25"], respectively, in the North Section finale Friday night. They won't be competing in Los Angeles during the coming weekend. As has happened in the past, Chico High officials are of the opinion that the clockings and marks recorded by the aforementioned trio are not up to the standards of the state meet, thus the cost of sending the young down south is not warranted.

Following college football, Charles Crabtree later served in the Army. After a brief career in banking, he moved home to Chico to start his own business, Charles Crabtree Painting Inc. Charlie, known for his generosity, kind heart, and loving spirit, passed on December 2, 2017.

POWELL FLY RODS

Chico has long been known as the "City of Trees," and for good reason. There are approximately 25,000 street trees within the public right of way in the city. Facilitating this tree growth are large quantities of fresh water provided by several creeks and a river. Big Chico Creek passes through the city and associated Sycamore, Mud, and Rock creeks lie a little to the north. Little Chico Creek also flows through the city; branching off it is Dead Horse and Edgar sloughs (the latter is also known as Comanche Creek). Creeks generally have flowing water, while sloughs may have little to no water flow and can be muddy or marshy. For boys in Chico, creeks offered opportunities for fishing; sloughs provided wildlife habitats but little recreational activities.) Butte Creek flows a little east of Chico and the Sacramento River forms the western boundary of farm and orchard lands just outside of Chico.

Rivers, creeks, and smaller streams in mountain watersheds to the north of Chico provided pristine recreational opportunities including fishing. Local fly fishermen, who regularly traveled to mountain streams in search of trout, could purchase Powell fly rods handcrafted in Chico. The story of three generations of Powells and their iconic product is taken up in the next chapter.

Photo 8-3

L-R: Walton Powell, Press Powell, and relatives Rich Powell and Eugene Powell at the Powell Fly Rod Shop.
Courtesy of The Powell Family

The third generation of Powell family fly rod craftsmen was Press Powell, a classmate and teammate of running back Tim O'Neill, quoted at chapter's head regarding the Chico High 1963 Football Team.

9

Powell Fly Rods

The Fisherman
Although I can see him still,
The freckled man who goes
To a grey place on a hill
In grey Connemara clothes
At dawn to cast his flies
It's long since I began
To call up to the eyes
This wise and simple man.

—First eight lines of "The Fisherman" by William Butler Yates.

The poem *The Fisherman* evokes a sense of nostalgia and connection to nature, portraying the fisherman as a man who lives in harmony with his environment. One who appreciates art and nature, contrasting him with the complexities of modern life and society.

Photo 9-1

Press Powell, of Chico Fly Shop (formerly Powell Fly Shop), demonstrating casting techniques at a fly-fishing workshop.
California State University, Chico *Orion*, April 14, 1993

Anyone who grew up in Chico in the 20th Century is likely familiar with, or at least knew of the existence of Powell Fly Rod Shop on West Eight Avenue. This business, which existed for decades until 2002, sold its famous rods locally to avid trout fishermen as well as to customers from all over the world. Press Powell, shown in the preceding photograph was a third-generation fly rod maker. Growing up in Chico he, like many of his peers, spent much of his leisure time enjoying sports and a variety of other activities in the great outdoors of northern California, including hunting and fishing.

Press's grandfather E.C. Powell started building handmade bamboo fly rods in Red Bluff, California, in the late teens/early 1920s. He later moved to a C Street shop in Marysville where he continued to make and sell rods. E.C. patented a type of semi-hollow bamboo rod construction, inspired by the fact that in those days tournament casting rods were entered into competition classes based on weight. A lighter rod capable of casting more line was advantagous.[1]

Photo 9-2

E.C. Powell.
Courtesy of The Powell Family

Few bamboo rods garnered as much attention, particularly in western circles, as those of E.C. Powell. (This interest remains today.) His company became known for high-end fly rod quality craftsmanship and that reputation and heritage continued as the business passed into the fiberglass era with E.C.'s son Walton Powell, then graphite era with Walton's son Press.[2]

Photo 9-3

Walton Powell: at left with a Grayling, and at right with a Steelhead trout.
Courtesy of The Powell Family

Photo 9-4

L-R: an E.C. Powell fly rod and one made by his son Walton Powell.
Courtesy of Rich Morrison

Walton worked primarily in three materials, bamboo, graphite, and fiberglass. After moving the business to Chico, he became known in the community for his innovative rod construction and for teaching others the magic of fly fishing. His role as Assistant Professor of Recreation at Chico State assisted in this endeavor. As indicated in an article in the *Wildcat* (following page), students could enroll in his evening fly fishing class. Benefits of paying the class fee of $48 included the use of knowledge gleaned in class during fishing trips.[3]

Complete Fly Fishing

This course will be an in-depth study of all phases of fly fishing including the fish, their habits and environment, stream and lake lore. There will be advanced lessons in fly tying, fly casting and fishing. Much of the time will be devoted to actual fishing on lakes and streams where conditions for demonstration of techniques are ideals. Fishing trips to be arranged.

Instructor: Walton E. Powell, Assistant Professor of Recreation.

Class meetings: Will meet for 5 weeks beginning Sept. 19, 1972 Every Tuesday and Thursday 7-9 p.m.

Location: Physical Science 109

Fee: $48.00

Registration: Students will register and pay fee at the first class meeting.

Course Code: 1029

For further information, contact: Office of Continuing Education, Chico State University, Chico, California, or telephone: 916-345-6106.

California State University, Chico *Wildcat*, September 20, 1972

When Press Powell eventually took over the shop on West Eighth Avenue, an abundance of legacy tributes to his father were displayed on the walls and elsewhere. These included:

- Walton Powell and his pipe-puffing pal Bing Crosby
- The women of the family tying award-winning flies
- In the family scrapbook, a note to Walt from former President Jimmy Carter referring to his "great experience" fishing and the fact that "we'll think of you each time we enjoy the beauty and design of the Powell Rods"
- A 1954 newspaper clipping calling Walton Powell simply, "Bamboo Rod man"
- A poster from the Robert Redford film *A River Runs Through It*, for which Walton was hired to consult and construct rods
- A copy of the letter from the state of Alaska granting him the first nonresident fishing license in history[4]

Press recalled about his father:

> He was a great teacher. He taught people the common-sense factor of fishing. I always felt that was my dad's greatest contribution in many, many ways. He was a great rod maker, but so much more important is that you help bring people into fly fishing.[5]

PHILLIP PRESS POWELL

Press spent most of his life in Chico, a town he loved. He graduated from Chico Senior High, Chico State, and obtained a Vocational Agriculture degree from the University of California, Davis. After teaching Vocational Agriculture at San Andreas High School for two years, and four years at Elk Grove High School, he returned to Chico in 1977 to join the family business of making fly fishing rods.[6]

While a junior at Chico State in 1968, Press was Delta Zeta's Irish Twirp King candidate. Twirp Week at Chico State involved women performing all the niceties for men that men usually do for women. These included girls paying for everything, and making goofy corsages for their dates at the week's concluding Twirp Dance.

Photo 9-5

Photo 9-6

Press Powell is pictured at left. The following year's Twirp King and Queen (Reed McLaughlin and Mary Jane Rivers) are pictured sharing a kiss, at right. Chico State College *Wildcat*, March 11, 1968, and Chico State yearbook *Record 1969*.

Press sold the Chico Fly Rod Shop in 2002 owing to ill heath. Sadly, he passed away on March 11, 2004 due to cancer.[7]

This account concludes with some insights by Press regarding fly fishing—his family's passion and longlasting legacy:

- Fly fishing promotes environmental awareness
- When you are out in the middle of the same stream at six in the morning, you begin to understand the interrelatedness of things in this world
- Too many people make fly fishing way more complicated than it really is

- Fly fishing is a series of fundamental skills to be taken one at a time[8]

ODE TO PRESS POWELL

> *Press was everybody's best friend. He had that ability to be in the moment and concentrate on who was before him; perhaps because he sincerely saw people as individuals and cared about them. Press's memory about people he'd met was incredible, and there were hundreds. He not only knew who your siblings were by name, but who your cousins were. Press recalled details lost to others, like where you worked last summer, and the layup you made to win the game in Marysville. He'd recite Kent Blevin's batting average and Teddy Gerber's time on the peg-board. Every one of his friends were extraordinary in their own way: Greg Toler was a maestro on the piano and would surely be famous one day; Mary Starmer could charm the socks off a blind banker; Pete Giampoli was so shrewd he'd own the town by the time he was out of college. Pete used to rib Press for being grandiose, but I'm not sure it was grandiosity so much as his positivity and loving over-exuberance about his friends.*
>
> —Tim O'Neill (Chico High Class of 1965) describing the enthusiasm of classmate and good pal, Press Powell.[9]

In addition to the above sketch about Press being a good friend to everyone, O'Neill also described his classmate's passion for fishing and a transformation of his normal demeanor when engaged in it:

> Press was proud of his name, his father and grandfather, but his love of fishing wasn't from loyalty or family vanity. Perhaps his obsession with the sport was initially genetic, but it was a chosen, not assigned, lifestyle.
>
> Press's exaggerated vitality appeared to mellow at the streambed. He'd give the trees and sky and stone their due reverence. He'd walk shallow water and cast his rod slowly, purposely, as if tuning a violin, catching the rhythm, the touch. And in that rhythm, he'd commune with God's graceful earth, the flowing of water and the fish swimming undetected until the perfect fly bumped its nose, placed there by a master fly caster. And the clouds would flow onward above us as the day warmed. I know, because I was there on the bank as Press prayerfully plied his craft.[10]

10

1965 Visit Home to Chico

I spent uncounted hours sitting at the bow looking at the water and the sky, studying each wave, different from the last, seeing how it caught the light, the air, the wind; watching patterns, the sweep of it all, and letting it take me.

—Gary Paulsen, *Caught by the Sea.*

When your ship is out to sea, operating independently—not steaming in a formation with other ships—all you see is water, sky and the horizon. If it is really foggy during the day or particularly dark at night with no moon, there might only be gray or blackness around you. It is quite an alone feeling. The vastness of the sea in comparison to a very small ship is humbling, and accents such feelings. Particularly while on deployment, I longed for letters from family, friends, and my girlfriend. It means a great deal to a serviceman to get word from home.[1]

During the early period of my time aboard *Hopewell*, I received a "Dear John" letter from my girlfriend in Chico. At mail call one day, I got a letter from her. Before I opened the letter, I said to myself that I would write her back and tell her that this letter was the best medicine I could have gotten for all my ailments. The letter started off, "Dear Mike, Ralph and I have been going steady for a month now." This was the same girl who had declared on more than one occasion, "I will love you forever!"[2]

Apparently forever had a short shelf-life. When you first embark on your Navy adventure, you expect to lose a few things as a result of your mom cleaning house and throwing away your prized baseball card and *Mad Magazine* collections, and hope that she didn't find the *Playboy* under the mattress. One thing you don't anticipate is losing your girl to some suave, sweet-talkin' guy with a hot car.[3]

Following the return of *Hopewell* from deployment to the Western Pacific and off Vietnam in February 1965, I spent some well-deserved leave in Chico. "It was the winter of '65; I was hungry and just barely alive," I can still hear those lyrics by Joan Baez in "The Night They Drove Old Dixie Down." It was actually February 1965, and not 1865, and I was home; time to get caught up with old friends, try to meet girls and do some serious drinkin'.[4]

While in Chico, I was now in the market for a date or two. No longer having my previous girlfriend, I was available for any and all girls in my home town, except, obviously, her. I made a few phone calls to girls with whom I had graduated from high school. Most were married or engaged. I also called a few girls from my sister's class, and what a surprise, I apparently was damaged goods due to the unpopularity of the war. There was an anti-war poster at this time that exclaimed "GIRLS SAY YES to boys who say NO," which I truly hated.[5]

Photo 10-1

Vietnam anti-war poster.

ITALIAN COTTAGE RESTAURANT

Advertisement in the Chico State College *Wildcat*, April 20, 1965.

One of the highlights of my visit to Chico was going out for a beer in my dress blues with a friend at a new restaurant, the Italian Cottage. The owners, Burt and Judy Katz, furnished me a gratis pitcher of beer. I have never forgotten that act of kindness they bestowed upon me, especially with the way that the general public treated us. While we were enjoying the beer, they informed me that because of the lack of customers they would probably have to go out of business. Given their financial situation, it must have been hard for them to give away that pitcher of beer. But they did it anyway.[6]

A few years later, I went by that location to see what had happened to the Italian Cottage, fully expecting to see another business in its place. To my great surprise the adjacent Signal gas station had been removed to make room for a parking lot to handle all the customers at a now thriving Italian Cottage. I guess karma is alive and well in the universe. The Italian Cottage is known for having the best pastrami sandwich north of San Francisco, and I will never forget the kindness extended to this serviceman.[7]

CHANGE OF TRADITIONAL RIVALS

In autumn 1965, the *Hopewell* was undergoing some much-needed work at the Long Beach Naval Shipyard, following return of the destroyer from deployment. While I was aboard her engrossed in the life of a sailor, a big change was occurring in Chico. Sophomore and juniors pulled from Chico High were beginning their school year at newly built Pleasant Valley High School. The next year, a large group of seniors left Chico High as well to join the earlier departed students now attending a crosstown competitor school. The following chapter, A Change of Traditional Rivals, tracks just one of the many talented, accomplished students lost by Chico High.

Photo 10-2

Pleasant Valley High School, home of the Vikings, Chico, CA.
1971-72 and 1970-71 *Valkyrie* yearbooks

PVHS Fight Song:

Come on and fight you Vikings win the game,
We're here to see our team take all the fame,
Go on to glory for our senior high,
And we will raise our banner to the sky tonight,
So clap and cheer them on so glorious,
Our Viking team will be victorious,
We'll shout for PV Senior High to win,
Fight on to Victory! Fight! Fight! Fight!

11

A Change of Traditional Rivals

Everyone in the entire northern state is watching us.

—Don Abbott, principal of Pleasant High School, addressing the 540 students who reported to the new school on September 7, 1965.[1]

Over the decades until the 1965-1966 school year opened at newly built Pleasant Valley High School (PV) in autumn 1965, Oroville High School (located in Oroville, twenty-five miles to the southeast) had been Chico High School's traditional rival. Henceforth, crosstown rival Pleasant Valley High would fill this role.

That said, PV was not initially at full strength. During its maiden year, the school handled only sophomores and juniors (540 students); all seniors remained at Chico High School. At Chico High School, 1,371 students in grades 10 through 12 now attended the proud institution. With the opening of Pleasant Valley High School, the school lost a large portion of its pupils. At one point during the previous school year, Chico High enrollment had been approximately 2,000 youths.[2]

The establishment of a second high school in Chico obviously provided benefits to the community. These included reduction of the strain on previously packed Chico High, and reduced travel distance to school for many students. Chico High School students shuttled off to Pleasant Valley High likely viewed this as either beneficial or detrimental depending on their personal circumstances and perspective.

There also was a weakening of Chico High's traditionally powerful sports teams owing to the loss of some of the community's best athletes to the new school. One such was Rob Laxson, son of Dr. C. Robert Laxson, a music professor at Chico State College from 1946 until his death in 1968. (On September. 25, 1974, University Auditorium was officially re-named Laxson Auditorium. This beloved Center of the Arts was originally named Assembly Hall during the inauguration ceremonies on January 22, 1932, and later became known as College Auditorium and then University Auditorium.)[3]

Rob attended Chico High his sophomore year (1964-65), and was a junior varsity three-sport athlete. He played football (quarterback), basketball (guard), and ran track (starting with the hurdles at his father's urging, ending as a quarter miler and relay team member). At season's finale in track, Laxson placed first in the quarter mile at the league championships and second in the North Section. His season best was 51.9 seconds. Notably, he was coached by three future Hall of Fame coaches: "Skip" McDonald and Mel Jones in football; Ken Piercy in basketball; and Mel Jones for track. (Francis "Skip" McDonald, Melvin R. "Mel" Jones, and Ken Piercy are all members of the Chico State Athletic and *Chico Enterprise-Record* Sports Halls of Fame.)

Photo 11-1

L-R: Coaches Mel Jones and "Skip" McDonald.
Chico High School yearbook *Caduceus '61*

Queried about his transfer to PV, and why he initially ran hurdles races in track, Laxson explained:

> I went to Pleasant Valley because we lived in their geographic area.
>
> My father was a hurdler and attended Ontario High School in Ontario, Oregon, and Monmouth College in Illinois. He did not ever talk much about his running, but I do remember him saying that he ran the 220 low hurdles at the Drake Relays and had the honor of running against the American record holder in that competition. [The Drake Relays is a prestigious track and field meet held annually at Drake Stadium in Des Moines, Iowa.]
>
> He never mentioned his place or time. My father's younger brother ran hurdles and long jumped and was the top individual scorer in the Oregon State High School Track Meet his senior year. If I had any speed at all it was from their family.[4]

After transferring to Pleasant Valley, Laxson lettered in these same sports his junior and senior years with expanded duties on the football team, and slight changes in events in track:

- Football (quarterback and flanker) – Coach Melvin R. "Bush" Dalrymple
- Basketball (guard) – Coach Edward "Doug" Kimbell
- Track & Field (880-yard run and relay member) – Coach Bill Skipper

Capping off the 1966 and 1967 Track & Field seasons, Rob was league and North Section champion in the half-mile race both years, with a personal best of 1:56.8 in the two-lapper.

MELVIN R. "BUSH" DALRYMPLE

Photo 11-2

"Skip" McDonald (left) and "Bush" Dalrymple (right) are pictured sitting side by side in this portion of the Chico State College 1948 Baseball Team photograph. The Wildcats were Far Western Conference champions.

Laxson, and other Viking students, was likely unaware of the impressive background of his football coach "Bush" Dalrymple, who in 1965 had become the Head Football Coach and Athletic Director at the newly constructed Pleasant Valley High.[5]

Melvin R. "Bush" Dalrymple grew up in Chico and attended local schools where he was a standout athlete. While attending Chico State, he played football and baseball and was awarded All-Conference honors in both sports, 1947 through 1950, and was selected as the Outstanding Senior Athlete in 1950.[6]

He enlisted in the U.S. Army in January 1952 and served in a tank battalion in the Korean Conflict where his vision was seriously damaged in battle. He was discharged in December 1953 and after some final college preparation, began his teaching career which lasted through his retirement in 1981.[7]

Dalrymple taught at Oroville, Chico Junior High, Chico High School, and Pleasant Valley High. He was inducted into the *Chico E-R* Sports Hall of Fame in 1978, the Chico State Athletic Hall of Fame in 1986, the Chico Baseball Legends of the Diamond in 2006, and in 1984 was named the Teacher of the Year by the Chico Unified Teachers Association. His passing on February 18, 2015 marked a great loss to the community.[8]

"Skip" McDonald (Dalrymple's baseball teammate at Chico State) enlisted in the Navy, following graduation from Red Bluff High School in 1944. At completion of his two-year hitch, he enrolled at Chico State College, where he was a three-sport stand-out athlete. Francis "Skip" McDonald passed away on May 4, 2017.

LAXSON ARRIVES AT OREGON STATE UNIVERSITY, JOINING CHICO HIGH GRADUATE GARY HOUSER PLAYING FOOTBALL END/WIDE RECEIVER

Former Chico Panther/Pleasant Valley Viking Rob Laxson attended Oregon State University in 1967-68 and ran track for the Beavers, before returning home and finishing his education at Chico State College. At least two other 1960s-era Chico High School graduates had previously attended and competed for Oregon State: Doug Parker in Track and Charlie Crabtree in Football. A third athlete from CHS was at OSU in autumn 1967 when Laxson arrived on campus: Gary Houser, a senior, who shortly thereafter would earn All-Conference honors in football.

OREGON STATE'S 1967 FOOTBALL TEAM

The 1967 Oregon State football team is arguably the most famous in history. Dubbed the "Giant Killers," the team was ranked No. 7 in the Associated Press Poll, No. 8 in the United Press International Poll. They finished with a 7-2-1 record, and tied for second in the conference.[9]

Early in the season, Oregon State earned the Giant Killer moniker by beating No. 1 ranked USC 3-0, No. 2 Purdue 22-14, and two weeks later playing UCLA, the new No. 2 ranked team, with a 16-16 tie. However, these soaring successes did not continue over the course of the season. Laxson recalled, "[We] beat USC and OJ Simpson 3-0 in the mud. That moved us up to 8th in the national polls, as we had also beaten Purdue with Mike Phipps and UCLA with Gary Beban, but the next week we got demolished by BYU and their air raid offense. That pretty much moved us from contender to pretender."[10]

OSU 3-0 VICTORY OVER USC, NOVEMBER 11, 1967

> *I remember that Saturday as a kid. The result shocked me. It was a battle of [USC's] Simpson and [OSU's Bill] "Earthquake" Enyart. They both went to the [NFL Buffalo] Bills. After watching the game, I can see why it was low scoring for sure. It looked as if the Beavers ground crew doused the middle of the field with a ton of water. It took away the Trojan speed.*
>
> —Recollection posted online from a viewer @wmontanez27 of a video of the football game on youtube.com.[11]

Probably the most unexpected Beavers football win, and perhaps the most satisfying that season, came against USC at home. As indicated in the quoted material, the general belief was that host Oregon State had purposely turned its football field into a mud pit in order to counter the speed and agility of Trojan running back OJ Simpson. In addition to OJ's prowess on the gridiron, he was also a track star. The following spring, USC's 4 x 100 relay team, led by Simpson, set the world record with a time of 38.6 seconds.

Beavers' Jon Sandstrom and Jess Lewis earned All-American honors that season. Bill Enyart, Gary Houser and Dave Marlette were Pac-8 All-Conference selections, and Enyart also an Academic All-American. Houser was selected as a Tight End. Houser is listed in the OSU 1966 and 1967 rosters as a wide receiver. He was a good blocker that didn't catch many passes because OSU did not throw that many passes. Houser also served as punter.[12]

At the 1968 AFL-NFL Draft held January 30-31, Houser (Height: 6-3 Weight: 225) was drafted in the 9th round (236th overall) by the New York Jets. Bad knees kept him out of the NFL.[13]

Following several post-OSU coaching stints, ex-Panther Gary Houser returned home in 1979, as defensive coordinator with Chico

State for 10 seasons, then took the reins as head coach from 1989 through 1996 when Wildcat football was eliminated.[14]

LAXSON A 4:08 MILER AT CHICO STATE

Rob Laxson began and ended his track career in Chico. A highlight was running 4:08.7 for the mile at the 1969 Far Western Conference Track & Field Championships. Duwayne Ray subsequently won the mile at the NCAA College Championships—becoming a national champion.

Photo 11-3

"Duwayne Ray, running with all the finesse of an outstanding runner, let highly regarded Bill Scobey from Humboldt State set the pace for the first three laps and most of the fourth until Scobey fell back. Then with 110 yards to go, he and teammate Rob Laxson put on a kick similar to the one they did against Hayward [State] and sprinted the entire distance like 440 yard relay anchor men to finish one, two in the event. Ray won it in a time of 4:08.5 and Laxson at 4:08.7, the best performance for the blond bomber."[15]

"Chico State proved to be number one and two in the mile with Duwayne Ray (foreground) and Rob Laxson first and second respectively winning the FWC event."[16]

Following graduation from Chico State, Rob Laxson coached Cross Country and Track & Field in Woodland, California, from 1972-1998. Starting at Woodland Jr. High, he moved on to Woodland High School. Laxson is a member of the Woodland Athletic Hall of Fame.

12

Waning Days Aboard *Hopewell*

Photo 12-1

The "Bear Hole" in upper Bidwell Park, Chico, California.

Aboard the destroyer *Hopewell*, when shipboard requirements were not consuming all my energy and attention, all I could think about was, when next I got home to Chico, getting a six-pack of beer and heading for the Bear Hole or Salmon Hole. These were the names of pristine swimming spots on a creek that ran through Bidwell Park. Bidwell Park, one of the largest municipal parks in the United States, encompasses miles of land stretching from the foothills into the heart of Chico. These spots along the creek were framed by volcanic lava rocks that channeled the crystal-clear water rushing down from the Cascade mountain range. I would dream of sunning myself on one of the big rocks with a trusty six-pack of Olympia, getting drunk and acting silly. If luck were with me, there would be unencumbered chicks present, and one would go home with me. Such are the dreams of a homesick sailor.[1]

On August 1, 1966, *Hopewell* returned home to San Diego. A few months later, she was sent to the Hunters Point Shipyard in South San Francisco, for an overhaul period. My remaining time aboard would be short because I had less than thirty days remaining of my enlistment.[2]

The ship's "retention officer," Electrician's Mate Chief Schneekloth, approached me with a proposal to "ship over," to re-enlist and stay in the Navy. After hearing about the benefits of "shipping over," I must admit that I was attracted by the $5,000.00 bonus.[3]

For a minute or so I thought about the '55 Chevy that I had seen on a car lot in Compton, California, and would have loved to purchase. However, I had aspirations to experience life outside the Navy. I declined to remain a sailor, and asked him not to be offended. This proved to be a good decision.[4]

Hunters Point was infamous for being a particularly dangerous neighborhood. While the *Hopewell* was in the yard in the fall of 1966, a sniper was on the loose, and people in the area were frightened of being his next victim. Standing at a bus stop with some other guys, the conversation turned to us all feeling that we had cross-hairs on us. This may sound crazy, but the feeling was real. Wariness permeated the area, as it did years later, when the Zodiac Killer was on the prowl. If the killer was ever caught, it occurred after we had left the yard.[5]

During the period while *Hopewell* was in the shipyard, I enjoyed a weekend liberty in Chico. I relished the visit home but found none of the fairer sex to spend time with before it was time to return to the ship. I made my way to the Greyhound bus station, on Wall Street in downtown Chico, waiting for the bus to San Francisco. After boarding, I found a seat next to a rather engaging young lady named Nancy. She and I shared a very enjoyable ride to San Francisco where she was attending a business college. We talked and laughed together. I later called her several times.[6]

She was always very pleasant and it seemed we had a lot in common. She finally informed me that she had a boyfriend in the Air Force. Having no luck with girls on leave and liberty, I devoted the remaining time I had left in the Navy to my duties aboard *Hopewell*.[7]

13

Return to College Life

I wanna go to a party school! Yeah, Chico State!

—Originator of statement unknown; sentiment very common.

Photo 13-1

Kendall Hall administration building.
Chico State College yearbook *Record 1967*

I was granted an early-out, allowed to leave active duty a little earlier than my actual date of separation, to enable me to return to Chico State College for the Spring Semester 1967. Dr. J. Russell Morris, a professor of education, had written a letter to Chico State on my behalf and was able to get me reinstated.[1]

The *Hopewell* transferred me to "separations" at Treasure Island in San Francisco Bay to be released from active duty. The officer in charge of supervising discharges decided that since I was a Yeoman I was to remain there an extra three weeks, typing discharge papers. His staff must have been short of clerical rates. I manned a trusty typewriter filling out discharge papers for the guys that left the ship with me and many others from other commands. I had some lighter moments, though. One sailor was a Native American with the last name of Screaming Eagle. However, the surname that took the prize was a Hospital Corpsman named Sick.[2]

Eventually, my time came and I boarded a Greyhound bus in San Francisco for Chico. I sat in the rear of the bus next to a window so that as I watched the landscape go by, I could snooze, relish my freedom, and fantasize what college would now be like. It turned out I was on the "milk run." The bus stopped at every small burg from San Francisco northward. But that was okay, I was on my way home.[3]

My reverie was soon interrupted when a very large red-headed woman, who was adorned with tattoos and had questionable hygiene, sat down next to me. She wanted to talk, so I sat there and I listened to her life story, which included her having been in prison. I wanted to be left alone and think about my impending return home after war duty, but did not tell her this. Before I got off in Chico, she told me her name and gave me her address; I did not pursue the invitation to stay in touch.[4]

COLLEGE LIFE AT CHICO STATE

> *I must study politics and war that my sons may have liberty to study mathematics and philosophy. My sons ought to study mathematics and philosophy, geography, natural history, naval architecture, navigation, commerce, and agriculture, in order to give their children a right to study painting, poetry, music, architecture, statuary, tapestry, and porcelain.*
>
> —John Adams, second president of the United States.

After returning to Chico, I found that I had changed, and so had the town. The girl that I had left behind was gone and so was my car (wrecked by a relative, a novice driver). I had grown up and so had Chico. My beautiful brick high school was soon torn down following a major earthquake in southern California due to fears that it might not survive a major tremor and was unsafe. Chico Senior High School was a gorgeous brick building with white marble gables and archways. Its large sweeping driveway led in from the Esplanade, the thoroughfare that ran in front of the school. In fact, the contractor hired to demolish it had a difficult time doing so with a wrecking ball. That proved the building had been the victim of an increasingly "safety conscious" society. Significantly, there are no major earthquake faults near Chico, and the school had stood proudly, unharmed by nature since 1920.[5]

Two other major projects had occurred in my absence: the construction of the world's largest earth-filled dam across the Feather River running through the nearby city of Oroville, and a freeway over Bidwell Park. Bidwell Park was the backdrop for the 1938 motion picture *Robin Hood*, starring Errol Flynn and Olivia de Havilland, filmed in Chico. This beautiful park was then the largest municipal park in the United States. Today, Bidwell Park is still the largest in America for a community the size of Chico. My hometown's other crown jewels are California State University, Chico, the second oldest public state college in California, and Sierra Nevada Brewery, one of the premier craft breweries in the United States.[6]

One of my first priorities upon returning to college was to learn how to do all the new dances with all the bitchin' moves that had come out while I was overseas. This would also be, I believed, a good way to get a girl. While registering for classes, I signed up for a physical education class that offered instruction on all the latest dances. I was feeling pretty good about this decision while walking back across campus. I was going to learn to do "The Swim," "The Monkey," and my all-time favorite "The Jerk."[7]

Photo 13-2

I took a class at Chico State to learn to "groove to" rock & roll music at party scenes, such as this one.

It just so happened that I was walking behind two girls who could not contain their glee at the possibility of a single guy in their dance class; the one for which I just signed up. As they continued their discussion I learned they wanted to see this guy in his leotards. Yikes, I had signed up for "art" dancing, or modern dance. I never made it to that class. I don't recall whether I dropped it, or just took an incomplete or "F" grade. All I know is that I never danced in tights.[8]

MORE MUNDANE ASPECTS OF COLLEGE LIFE

Upon arriving back in Chico, I moved into an apartment with a guy I had known since our time in second grade at Chapman School in 1950. Robert Vanderley lived a block away and we went to the same schools and both graduated in 1961 from Chico High School. He had been in the Navy as a Dental Technician at Naval Air Station Whidbey Island (about 30 miles north of Seattle), and I had served on a destroyer.

We were roommates on East Sixth Street. The apartment had been occupied by my best friend, Bruce Wadlington, while I was overseas. A young red-headed girl moved in next door and that was enough for me to date her for two years.

I knew that I needed books and some cash to attend Chico State. Someone told me that you needed a slide rule. So, being a prepared student, I bought a slide rule in a cool leather scabbard. It fastened to my belt. You guessed it. I never used it and I never wore it again. I wonder whatever happened to it. Maybe it was one of those things that your mom throws away (or gives away) when you enter the service.

As a student you needed your books. I wish that I had remembered what Benjamin Franklin said about the mother of invention - necessity - because I carried an arm full of books to college from our house about three miles away. That's carrying them to school and then back home. College students didn't have lockers like in high school. Maybe that's why I have a sore back in the mornings.

DRAMATIC CHANGES AT CHICO STATE IN 1968

Bob Dylan's song "The Times They Are a-Changin" was the title track on his third studio album released on February 10, 1964, through Columbia Records. He accurately prophesied the times. Cultural and social change that spurred the timeless protest song became readily apparent in 1968 on the Chico State campus. This took the form of an anti-war rally and other unrest on campus and, for the first time, San Francisco-based bands (reflecting a mixture of Bay Area psychedelics, rock 'n' roll and rebellion) being brought to Chico State to perform.

14

Protest Against the Draft in 1968

[I]t seems now more certain than ever that the bloody experience of Vietnam is to end in stalemate… [I]t is increasingly clear to this reporter that the only rational way out then will be to negotiate, not as victors, but as an honorable people who lived up to their pledge to defend democracy, and did the best they could.

—News anchorman Walter Cronkite in CBS (Columbia Broadcasting System) "Report from Vietnam: Who, What, When, Where, Why," which aired on 27 February 1968. The excerpt came at the end of the hour-long special, which Cronkite acknowledged was subjective, his opinion.[1]

TET PROVES TO BE TURNING POINT IN THE WAR

On 29 January 1968 in the Republic of Vietnam, Allied forces began the Tet-lunar new year expecting the customary 36-hour peaceful holiday truce. Such was not to be. Capitalizing on the lull in war posture, the North Vietnamese and Viet Cong launched a large-scale offensive on targets across South Vietnam. Assaults began in the northern and central provinces prior to dawn on 30 January, followed by ones that night in Saigon and the Mekong Delta regions. Enemy forces attacked or fired upon scores of provincial capitals, autonomous cities, district capitals, and hamlets, and raided a number of military installations including almost every airfield.[2]

Although U.S. and South Vietnamese forces managed to hold off the attacks on more than 100 cities and outposts in South Vietnam, news coverage of the massive Tet Offensive shocked the American public and eroded support for the war effort. Despite heavy casualties, North Vietnam achieved a strategic victory, as the attacks marked a turning point in the Vietnam War and the beginning of the slow, painful American withdrawal from the region.[3]

The Tet Offensive had a profound impact on college campuses across America, including at Chico State. While the offensive itself was a failure on the battlefield, it proved to be an astounding success at the bastions of higher education, where it sparked widespread protests and demonstrations. The anti-war movement and the draft lottery system, already prevalent concerns for American youth, became much more so as the public's viewpoint of the war shifted from positive to negative.

The day after anchor Walter Cronkite's "Report from Vietnam: Who, What, When, Where, Why" aired on the CBS evening news on February 27th, an Anti-Draft Rally was held at Chico State.

Anti-Draft Rally

CSC Instructor Tears Up His Draft Card

Photo 14-1

Anti-war rally on Chico State campus.
Chico Enterprise-Record, February 29, 1968

On Wednesday, February 28, 1968, over 800 gatherers heard 10 persons speak against U.S. draft laws in a rally on the Chico State College (CSC) campus. Several CSC instructors spoke, as well as two Chico professional men and a visiting member of the Berkeley Resistance. One of the CSC instructors present tore up his draft card; another vowed he would not serve if drafted.[4]

Retired Chico State music professor David Rothe recalled in an interview that the "hip crowd" began to show up in 1969 and 1970. He described two examples of student protest on the campus:

> They made an attempt to remove the flag from the front of the administration building as a war protest. The agriculture students and the veterans showed up to put an end to that protest. Curiously, the local issue which seemed to get everyone's attention was the closure of [West] First Street. The 'Chico Fifteen' staged a sit-in—to close First Street—and the National Guard was called in. As crowds gathered to observe this scene, members of the Chico State Band worked the crowd selling candy bars to support their band tour to Victoria, Canada.[5]

THE CHICO FIFTEEN

Photo 14-2

Members of the Chico 15 in a mock football team formation. Front line (left to right) – Dan Chandler, Tom Hearn, Nick Blake, Dan Trevithick and Frank Burk; backfield (left to right) – Steve Thornton, Sandra Rothacker, Paul Morgan, Mike Rice, Jack Zeilinga, Kathleen Shelter and Kevin Campbell. Not shown are Ken Pepper, Tom Edwards, and Kurt Staib.
Chico State College *Wildcat*, May 27, 1970

On April 22, 1970, students celebrating the first Earth Day on the Chico State campus shoved a car into West First Street (which was then State Route 32) blocking traffic. The incident escalated into a demonstration that lasted into the night, resulting in the street being closed temporarily for safety. The protesters ("Chico 15") were arrested on conspiracy charges which were later dropped. The street re-opened the following day; but was permanently closed over the segment running through campus later that year.[6]

The infamous "Chico Fifteen" was initially identified in *Wildcat* articles at the Chico Sixteen, but apparently Tom Edwards had erroneously been identified as a member of the group. Fifteen individuals were listed in an article titled "Chico '15' finally wins one round," published in the *Wildcat* on October 2, 1970. The article reported in part:

> On Sept. 29 the Third District Court of Appeal in Sacramento granted attorneys representing the Chico 15 a writ of prohibition, thus stopping their Butte County Superior Court trial which was scheduled to begin Nov. 2.

Some reading this account today might be wondering what the big deal was about protestors temporarily closing West First Street? The answer is that today, what is a lightly travelled street over the portion of campus that remains open was then a major thoroughfare of Chico.

A *Wildcat* article titled "City may close First Street" (published on April 17, 1970) began with, "There are over 9,000 students at Chico State and nearly all cross First Street at least twice a day. Where were all of you Tuesday night?" This rebuke referred to low attendance at a public hearing held by the Chico City Council on the campus concerning the closing of First between Salem and Ivy streets.

The article cited, "6,000 cars travel First daily and anywhere from 20,000 to 30,000 pedestrians cross the street," highlighting danger of the current situation. It also summarized competing interests, and the estimated cost to close the street on campus:

> Objections to the closure ranged from "look at the number of parking places to be lost" to "you give them one street, they'll just want another" but the major complaint was simply monetary. One individual at the hearing figured the cost of First Street and adjacent Hazel, Chestnut, and Normal between First and Second which would also have to be closed if First was, to be over a half million dollars and the college would have to pay this amount.

Nothing was decided at the meeting on April 14th. It ended with the parties involved at an impasse—eight days later the Chico Fifteen sprang into action.

15

Concerts at Chico State in the late 1960s

A special memory for me was coming into Acker [North Gym] after football practice and the entire team being treated to a 45 minute "Mike check" from Harry Belafonte. General manager of students Mack Martin was instrumental in bringing "high quality" entertainers to this community.

—Former Wildcat Sam Simmons recalling Harry Belafonte singing during equipment checks before his show later that evening, November 22, 1966. Supporting showmen Nipsey Russell and Nana Mouskouri also performed that night.[1]

High culture was virtually non-existent in Chico. Rock or even guitar were virtually unknown in the music department. The Music Department was very conservative in those days. Everybody wore white shirts with skinny little ties.

—Retired music professor David Rothe describing the conservative nature of the Chico State music department when he began his tenure at the college in January 1968.[2]

Prior to 1968, Chico State had long brought well known entertainers to perform on campus, but they were largely non-controversial artists like singer Harry Belafonte who popularized calypso music. But, by the late 1960s, there were pockets of students at Chico State that gravitated to the revolutionary culture taking place in San Francisco. Perhaps as a result, music groups began performing in Chico that were a part of the San Francisco music scene—a mixture of psychedelics, rock 'n' roll and rebellion colored with paisley and tie-dye.[3]

These included in 1968, Big Brother and the Holding Company, and the Grateful Dead, and later the Doobie Brothers, and Oakland's Tower of Power (R&B, Funk and Soul Band). Providing a diversity of music for Wildcat concert goers in 1968-69 were national artists of other genres passing through northern California. These included Lou Rawls, The Fifth Dimension, Joan Baez, and Johnny Cash.

Although most of these bands/artists performed in the North Gym or College Stadium at Chico State, some events were held in the Armory Building at the Silver Dollar Fairgrounds or other locations.

SOUL SINGER LOU RAWLS

Kicking off 1968, Lou Rawls, one of the top soul singers on the nightclub circuit, appeared in concert at 8:15 pm in the North Gym on January 18, 1968. The concert was the latest in the Performing Arts series sponsored by the College Union Program Council.[4]

Rawls who was from Chicago, got his start singing there. In 1955, he enlisted in the United States Army and was a paratrooper in the 82nd Airborne Division. He served in B Co 2/505th Parachute Infantry and at the conclusion of his three years, left the Army as a Sergeant.[5]

Photo 15-1

Singer Lou Rawls.
Chico State College *Wildcat*, January 5, 1968

Rawls began his recording career with "Stormy Monday" in 1961, and followed it with numerous other albums. Two of his most popular songs were "Dead End Street" and "St. Louis Blues." In 1967, he won a Grammy Award for Best R&B Vocal Performance for the single "Dead End Street." It was the first of three Best Male R&B Vocal Performance Grammy Awards he earned during his career.[6]

THE FIFTH DIMENSION

Chico State students reading the Monday, February 12, 1968 issue of the *Wildcat* learned via an article titled, "The 5th Dimension Coming Thursday Night" the group would be performing three days later. The Fifth Dimension was one of the most successful vocal groups of the late 1960s and early 1970s, producing classic songs like "Aquarius/Let the Sunshine In," "Up, Up and Away," and "Wedding Bell Blues."[7]

Originally formed in 1966 in Los Angeles, the group blended soul, pop, and psychedelic sounds with stunning vocal harmonies—not surprising, considering that the group's original lineup collectively won 33 Grammies during their careers:

- Marilyn McCoo – 8 Grammy Awards
- Billy Davis Jr. – 7 Grammy Awards
- Florence LaRue – 6 Grammy Awards
- Lamonte McLemore – 6 Grammy Awards
- Ron Townson – 6 Grammy Awards[8]

BIG BROTHER AND THE HOLDING COMPANY

Photo 15-2

Band members: Peter Albin (band leader and bassist), Dave Getz (drummer), Sam Andrew (guitarist), James Gurley (guitarist), and lead singer Janis Joplin. (Members' order of identification do not correspond with their positions in photo.) Chico State College *Wildcat*, May 4, 1968

In spring 1968, Big Brother and the Holding Company played College Stadium at Chico State on Wednesday, May 8th. One of the West Coast's top hard-rock attractions, the band was best known for singer Janis Joplin, who joined the group as lead vocalist in 1966. Formed in San Francisco in 1965, the band had quickly gained a following in the Bay Area music scene with their high-energy performances and improvisational style.[9]

A year earlier in 1967, the band had released their self-titled debut album, which included the hit single "Down on Me." Their second album, "Cheap Thrills," featuring Janis Joplin on vocals, brought them widespread recognition. "Cheap Thrills" reached number one on the Billboard charts. It included the hit songs "Piece of My Heart" and "Summertime."[10]

Despite Big Brother and the Holding Company's great success, friction developed in the band and Joplin left the group in 1968 to pursue a solo career. The band continued to perform and record, but were never able to recapture the success they had achieved with her as their lead vocalist.[11]

Dan Casamajor (whose father Gordon was then mayor of Chico) was at the Big Brother and the Holding Company concert which drew some 4,500 people. He later recalled about the event, "I was virtually at the stage. Janis was clearly taking frequent nips at a pint of Southern Comfort that she had with her (violating the dry-campus rule)."[12]

THE GRATEFUL DEAD

Photo 15-3

The Grateful Dead band members.
Chico State College *Wildcat*, November 1, 1968

That autumn, the Grateful Dead played in the Armory Building at the Silver Dollar Fairgrounds on November 1st. The American rock jam band had been formed in 1965 in Palo Alto, California. It epitomized the improvisational psychedelic music that flowered in and around San Francisco in the mid-1960s. Its original members were lead guitarist and vocalist Jerry Garcia, guitarist and vocalist Bob Weir, keyboard player Ron McKernan, bassist Phil Lesh, and drummer Bill Kreutzmann.

Known for its eclectic style which fused many different types of music together, The Grateful Dead was one of the most successful touring bands in rock history; one which, despite having virtually no radio hits, developed a large, devoted fan base, known as "Deadheads."

JOAN BAEZ

Photo 15-4

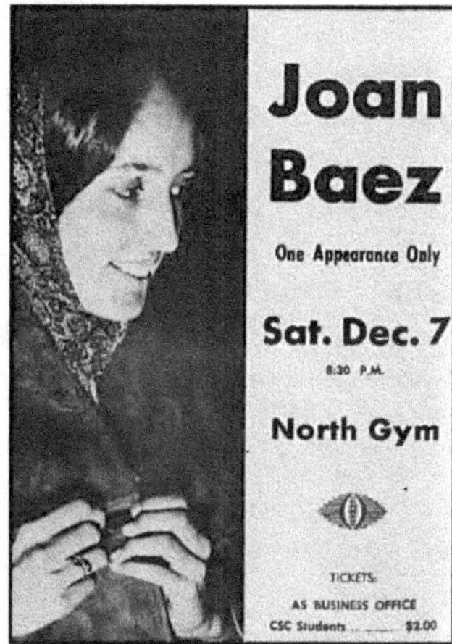

Singer Joan Baez.
Chico State College *Wildcat*, November 25, and December 9, 1968

Well known folk singer and activist Joan Baez performed in the North Gym at Chico State on December 7th. After beginning her recording career in 1960, she achieved immediate success with her first three albums, "Joan Baez," "Joan Baez, Vol. 2" and "Joan Baez in Concert," achieving gold record status. Although a songwriter herself, Baez generally interpreted others' work. She was one of the first major artists to record songs by Bob Dylan in the early 1960s.

Pat Kopp, Chico State's retired director of University Public Events, recalled Baez's December 1968 performance as being terse:

> The young folk singer "got upset because someone took her picture. She shortchanged the audience, playing 20 or 25 minutes."[13]

Rick Foster, a 1968 Chico State graduate, also attended Baez's Vietnam War-era show in the North Gym.

> It was packed. I forget the opening act, but when Baez came out to sing, she just sat on a stool at center court and alternately sang and talked. Her talk was about political issues, mainly the war and attempts to protest against the war. That suited me, but it was clear that some people felt the balance between music and political talk was too skewed toward talk.[14]

Following her three-hour performance, Baez talked with reporters in the "visiting team" locker room of the North Gym. Excerpts from an article titled "Singer still digs pacifism" published in the *Wildcat* on December 9, 1968 follow:

> Miss Baez said she didn't see how her arrest and imprisonment several months ago for an anti-draft sit-in had changed her image or hurt her career as she had always been "a risk." Basically, she feels her public stance hasn't changed, but because she's cut her hair the press is listening more closely to what she is saying....
>
> In order to prevent a "Big Casino" (world war) from occurring, she feels Gandhi's method of passive resistance is the answer.
>
> "After 5,000 years of war and violence," she said, "this man of India finally started something new that worked."

JOHNNY CASH, MARTY ROBBINS, AND OTHERS

Photo 15-5

Left: Johnny Cash, and right: Johnny Cash and Marty Robbins promotional ad. Chico State College yearbook *Record 1969* and the *Wildcat*, February 10, 1969

Continuing its support of a diversity of music, Chico State brought Country Western music royalty to the campus in early 1969. Johnny Cash and Marty Robbins were the headliners, with Carl Perkins, the Statler Family and the Carter Family also performing on February 25th.[15]

The cost of tickets was, $4 (Reserved), $3 (General Admission), and $2 (CSC Students).[16]

16

Student Body Largely Focused on Studies

Chico was divided. Often at noon there was political talk in front of the CAC (now the BMU) sponsored by one or another group opposed to the war. Occasionally hecklers showed up, but were pretty marginalized. Only small crowds stayed around for the anti-war discussions too so it was like only a few were committed on each side. Most students just were not that involved.

—Rick Foster, a 1968 Chico State graduate who retired to Durango, Colorado, after teaching political science in Idaho for 35 years, explaining that neither the Chico hippies nor the straight folks made a huge amount of noise in 1968.[1]

During my time as an art major at Chico State, much of my time was spent in the art building at the southeast corner of the campus adjacent to downtown. The PE Department (and associated locker rooms, gym, stadium and athletic fields) was located in the northwest area adjacent to railroad tracks running through town. Picturesque Big Chico Creek bisects the campus, so students used a footbridge to gain access to these and other campus buildings and facilities.

Photo 16-1

Little green footbridge over Big Chico Creek allowed Chico State students to move between the main campus and buildings on the other side of the picturesque creek. Chico State College yearbook *Normal Record 1947*

The campus was relatively small, and it was easy to roam wherever necessary or desired. I took a football physical education class from George Maderos, arguably the finest all-around athlete ever produced by Chico High School and Chico State College (CSC). He'd been hired by CSC after an injury ended his professional football career with the San Francico 49ers. More about him follows in a chapter devoted to Chico State Boxing. Coach Maderos was assistant to legendary coach Willie Simmons, whose "smokers" were well known on campus. Held each winter immediately preceding boxing season, novices had opportunity to venture into a ring set up in the North Gym. Students whose pugilistic skills were sufficiently impressive at "Willie Simmons' Smokers," had opportunity to make the team. These events were very well attended by Chico State students—there to watch the action, not to fight.

Photo 16-2

Chico State Football Coach George Maderos.
Chico State College yearbook *Record 1967*

"Greek Life," referring to the collective organization of fraternities (men) and sororities (women) that are often identified by Greek letters, was popular on campus. These organizations played a significant role in college culture across America, with a mission of fostering lifelong friendships, leadership skills, and community involvement.

I was a member of Alpha Phi Omega, founded in 1925 at Lafayette College in Easton, Pennsylvania, by Frank Reed Horton who had served in the U.S. Navy during World War I. Having finished my Navy enlistment as a Yeoman Second Class Petty Officer and, accordingly, being proficient with a typewriter, I was drafted as required for fraternity correspondence duties.

Photo 16-3

Alpha Phi Omega serves people

Alpha Phi Omega upheld its long-standing reputation as Chico State's most active service fraternity with another busy year.

In the fall, the members sponsored a campus blood drive for a local hemophiliac that netted over 100 pints. They also organized Butte County Sheriff Larry Gillick's food and toy drive at Christmas.

The club also maintains a huge sign downtown that advertises college and community events.

In the spring, APO sponsored a benefit dance for mentally retarded children.

The members also lead tours of the campus for visitors.

Mike Halldorson, arm bandaged after his own donation, helps out with the blood drive's paper work.

Chico State student and Alpha Phi Omega Fraternity member Michael Halldorson. Chico State College yearbook *Record 1969*

I had transportation to get around town compliments of my brother Alan who had joined the Navy in October 1968. During his absence, he allowed me to use his car. In his letters home, Alan would periodically inquire about his '57 Chevy. He knew that it had some serious wiring problems. (I occasionally had to have someone push it to help me get it started.) He also wondered if I liked the eight-track tapes that he had left in the car. Two of them were by Credence Clear Water Revival. I recall one of their songs in particular, "Fortunate Son." A part of the lyrics are: "It ain't me, it ain't me, I ain't no senator's son. It ain't me, it ain't me. I ain't no fortunate one, no." Many, if not most, of the men and women who went off to war were proud to serve. However, there was some resentment among draftees, who felt that they were not fortunate sons.[2]

Alan served aboard the tank landing ships *Caddo Parish* (LST-515) and *Iredell County* (LST-839) in inland waters of the Republic of Vietnam.

He was released from active duty in April of 1970 and thereafter went to work for the family appliance repair business in Chico.[3]

Photo 16-4

'57 Chevy.
Chico State College *Wildcat*, February 15, 1957

In addition to spending leisure time involved with Greek social activities, or enjoying night life in Chico establishments, students could engage in a plethora of outdoor activities. These included school sports teams and intramural sports. Associate professor Garth Dunning, who readers will learn more about in the following chapter, was the director of the intramural program, as well as coach of the skiing and gymnastics teams.

For many years, Garth, assisted by Political Science and Journalism Professor Jim Gregg (also a proficient skier), would take students up to a little ski area above Truckee over spring break to teach them skiing. This was not the ski team Garth coached. It was a course in which students could get one unit of credit for learning how to ski in the Lake Tahoe area. Gregg served as a Navy Photographer's Mate 3rd Class during the latter part of World War II, flying in the back seat of Douglas SBD-3 Dauntless dive bombers as an aerial photographer. He maintained a love for the outdoors and photography throughout his life, and further explored this through piloting and being part owner of a Laister LP-49 high-wing, single-seat, glider.[4]

17

Chico State College's Unconventional Ski Program

Garth Dunning's 1962 Wildcat ski team won the first intercollegiate ski meet ever for Chico State. The skiers swept all four team events at the Vanderbilt Memorial races at Squaw Valley against California [UC Berkeley] and Sierra College.

Chico State hosted California, Nevada, Arizona State, Sierra College and College of the Siskiyous at the third annual Chico State Invitational Ski Meet held this year at the Donner Ski Ranch. Nevada took top honors and the Governor's cup at the CSC meet.

—Chico State College yearbook *Record 1962.*

Photo 17-1

A fine jump by Wildcat ski team member Bob Lockey.
Chico State College yearbook *Record 1965*

Visitors to Chico in the 1960s, who had occasion to pass by the athletic fields at Chico State, may well have done a double-take upon sighting a ski jump far from any source of snow. It and other supporting facilities were the brainchild of Chico State ski coach Garth Dunning as detailed in an article titled "Skiers Need No Snow to Ski" published in the Chico State College *Wildcat* on November 21, 1961:

> Flashing down the ski jump, a Chico State ski team member plummets earthward. Far below, the cross country skiers are tramping over their course with determined concentration. A mile away, another fifty skiers are practicing their skills.
>
> Not an unusual sight you may say, unless you are at Chico in the Sacramento Valley and there is no snow on the ground.
>
> Garth Dunning's CSC ski team members are not letting the lack of snow on the California ski slopes delay their preparations for the coming season.
>
> Dunning and the ski team have erected a [practice] ski jump on the east side of the [roof of the] old gym, enabling them to make practice jumps of up to 40 feet.
>
> The structure was built from donated lumber and materials, and is covered with artificial fiberglass snow. Dunning states that the fake snow is even faster than the real stuff.
>
> The ski team also has a simulated cross-country course made of heavy canvas. The circular course allows team members to work-out without having the real thing under their skis.
>
> Dunning says that the team plans to make its first wet runs during Christmas vacation at Squaw Valley. If the snow conditions aren't satisfactory, they will head north to Utah.

As stated above, the ski jump was initially located behind Bidwell Mansion on the roof of the original gymnasium. This old gym was torn down, replaced by the Education/Psychology building in 1961. The new Art Acker Gym was built on Warner Street. In 1963, the ski team received permission to build a replacement 60-foot, stand-alone ski jump on the northwest corner of the CSC athletic fields (where West Sacramento Avenue crosses the railroad tracks).

For those who know that several years at a time can pass without even a sprinkling of snow in Chico, the sight of a ski jump on the college campus might beg the question, "how do the skiers land safely?" The answer is, a bed of cushed almond shells which nicely absorbed the force of impact.

Almond trees (predominant in Chico and other communities in California's central valley that collectively account for 80 percent of the world's supply) yield three products. Besides the almond kernels, protective hulls and shells account for about 70 percent of almond nut weight. Hulls and shells once removed from the nuts, are mostly used as an ingredient for cattle feed but, as this example shows, can also be utilized for other things.

Photo 17-2

Wildcat team captain Herb Scott showing beautiful form while launching from the campus practice jump at sunset. Chico State College yearbook *Record 1962*

TRAGIC LOSS OF DUNNING AND FARMER

Associate professor of Physical Education Garth Dunning was born in Chico on December 18, 1927. Chico State's intrepid and inventive first ski coach died on August 5, 1969 at age 41. Dunning was presumed drowned in a scuba diving outing in the deep frigid waters of Lake Tahoe with Jack S. Farmer (a June 1969 graduate of Chico State), who was also lost and presumed dead. As reported in a Chico State College *Wildcat* article titled "PE department hit by summer tragedy:"

> The accident occurred at Crystal Bay, Lake Tahoe about 100 yards offshore. Both men were experienced in diving with scuba equipment. Choppy water hampered [Coast Guard] search efforts.[1]

> Neither body was recovered.[2]

Photo 17-3

Chico State College ski instructor Garth Dunning.
Chico State College yearbook *Record 1960*

POSTHUMOUS HALL OF FAME MEMBER

In 1987, Garth Dunning was inducted into the Chico State Athletic Hall of Fame posthumously. He was a versatile, well accomplished Wildcat athlete before being hired by Chico State as its ski team and gymnastics coach, and director of intramural athletics.[3]

GARTH DUNNING, Chico (Awarded posthumously)
Boxing: 1949, 50, 51, 52
Invited to 1952 Olympic boxing trials. Member of ski team, tumbling and gymnastics team. Director of intramural athletics, ski team coach, and gymnastics coach at Chico State. His 1963 ski team took 1st place at the Winter Carnival. Officiated and assisted ski jumping and cross country events at the 1960 Winter Olympics at Squaw Valley.

Dunning lettered in boxing 1949-1952 while an athlete at Chico State, and had been invited to the 1952 Olympic boxing trials. The next chapter is devoted to this longtime favorite sport at Chico State.

18

Chico State Boxing

I cannot express enough thanks and gratitude to Willie Simmons and George Maderos, our two boxing coaches. Both of these gentlemen were very good athletes in their days. They promoted fitness, competition, and fun through fitness for life. In some way, they were also like an extended father figure. I will never forget them. Also, I cannot discount the boxing connection we had with Mel Jones, either. He was our high school track coach who also participated in boxing in his earlier years. [Jones lettered in baseball, track, and boxing while attending Chico State, becoming a Far Western Conference boxing champion in 1950.]

—Pat Buzbee.

Photo 18-1

Chico State Boxing team in the early 1970s. Mike Buzbee is in the top row, second from the left, and Pat Buzbee is below him in the front row.
Courtesy of Pat Buzbee

Chico State's North Gym (renamed Art Acker Gym) was a hub of activity during and after classes. Here, students took PE courses, participated in Wildcat/intramural sports, listened to speakers invited to campus, and attended music concerts with entertainers like Ike and Tina Turner, the Doobie Brothers, Janis Joplin and others.

Firstly, the North Gym was the domain of the school's coaches/PE instructors. Among this group were two legends, Willie Simmons and

George Maderos. Among the sports they coached was boxing. Both were later inducted into the *Chico Enterprise-Record* Sports Hall of Fame and the Chico State Athletic Hall of Fame. Sadly, both passed in 2017; Simmons at the age of 98, and Maderos at 83.

William T. "Willie" Simmons' enlistment in World War II brought him to the Chico Base of the Army Air Force. Following the war, Willie enrolled at Chico State where he competed in four sports, lettering multiple times in each, and was student body president. In addition to the BA Degree in Physical Education, which he earned at Chico State, he later added a Master's Degree from Chico State in 1951 and a Doctor of Education Degree from the University of Oregon in 1963. During his long tenure at Chico State from 1953 to 1989, Willie coached football, boxing, track, and cross country.[1]

Photo 18-2

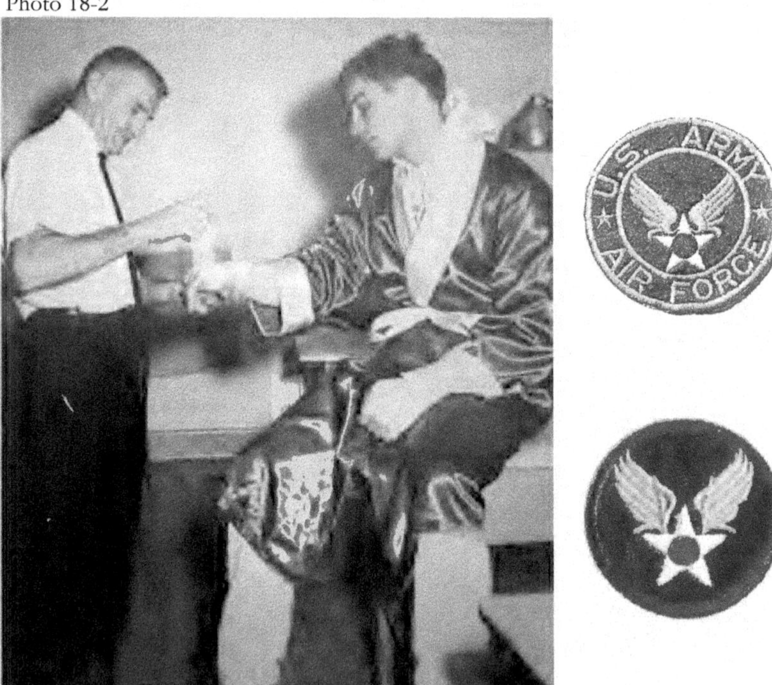

Coach Willie Simmons taping the hands of a fighter before a boxing match.
Chico State College yearbook *Record 1967*

George Maderos starred for Chico State in the early 1950s, competing in football, basketball, boxing and track and field while lettering 14 times, more than any other athlete in school history. Orrin "Skip" Reager, a former Sports Editor at the *Enterprise-Record* and member of both the Chico State and Chico Sports Halls of Fame, observed about him, "Without a doubt, George is the greatest athlete ever to come out of Chico State." The Chico native went on to play professional football for the San Francisco 49ers for two years before returning to the community he loved, and accepting a position at Chico State. Maderos was head coach for football (10 years), boxing (4) and track teams (1) during a 38-year teaching career at the school.[2]

Boxing was very popular at Chico State for a host of reasons. These included the draw of coaches Simmons and Maderos; the sport's proud tradition that extended back decades at the college; and because boxing was taught in PE classes at Chico High School. Pleasant Valley High School may have also offered boxing. In any case, these local high schools developed many athletes that attended Chico State.

Among them were twins Pat and Mike Buzbee, 1969 Chico High School graduates, who began their freshman year at Chico State that fall. Their introduction to Wildcat boxing came on December 16th, when they fought each other during an intramural match. This short chapter provides snippets of their 1972 and 1973 boxing seasons. While most boxers do some "roadwork" to improve their endurance, Pat and Mike were competitive distance runners who boxed. Both ran a marathon race in under two hours, thirty minutes. When asked about how two runners took up boxing, Pat Buzbee quipped, "who would not want to be coached by Willie Simmons?"

Chico State College's 1972 boxing season under Simmons and Maderos began on Thursday, January 6th with the annual "Bash" in the North Gymnasium. The varsity team was to open its California Collegiate Boxing Conference season on Saturday, January 15th, at University of Nevada-Reno. Bouts in the "Bash" were designed to help determine which boxers would be selected to make the trip. Highlighted in a *Chico Enterprise-Record* article the previous day (titled "CSC Boxers to Battle in Annual Bash Tomorrow") was that three sets of brothers would be participating:

> Two sets of twins and a third brother act highlight this year's "Bash."
>
> Pat and Mike Buzbee will face new opponents after fighting it out themselves the past two winters.
>
> Also boxing will be Jim and Tom Guyn but they will not face each other.
>
> Veteran Stan Parrish will meet younger brother Desmond.

A *Chico E-R* article the following day cited that a crowd of approximately 2,000 spectators had been present in North Gymnasium the previous night as Simmons and Maderos sent their beginning, advanced and veteran boxers into action in the annual "Bash." "Most of those on hand were students and they were impressed by the fisticuffs presented in the 13 bouts."

The Chico State boxing team lost to host Nevada-Reno in its season opener by a score of 9½ - 3½. (The winner of a boxing match garners 1 point; ½ point signify a draw between opponents.)

There being very few northern California university/college boxing programs at that time, Chico State competed against University of California, Berkeley (Cal), University of Nevada-Reno, and a U.S. Navy team based in the San Francisco Bay Area. Most of Chico's boxing matches were against Cal and Nevada-Reno.

Chico would next take on Cal-Berkeley, with Pat Buzbee making his first start of the season, representing the Wildcats at the 125-pound weight class. (Weighing maybe 112 pounds, Pat, not unexpectedly, generally liked to fight at the lowest weight class, 118 pounds. However, for this and other fights, whichever Buzbee twin was "given the nod" they fought where placed on the card.)

Chico prevailed against Cal on January 22, 1972. The result of Pat Buzbee's bout was reported in the *Enterprise-Record* on January 24, 1972 under the headline "Wildcat Boxers Trim Bears 10-4 in CCBC":

> Pat Buzbee started the Chico win parade, but Pat, going to the post for the first time this season, had to storm back from a rocky first round as opponent Bob Guimarin got off to an early lead.
>
> The taller Bear boxer scored well in the initial heat, but Pat turned the tide in the second with straight right hand leads then opened up in the third to stop his tiring foe with 20 seconds remaining in the final round.

The next boxing match was also against Cal. The program (shown below) for the February 13, 1972 meeting listed "Mike or Pat Buzbee" once again matched against Bob Guimarin, but this time at 132 pounds. It appears that Guimarin unable to make 125 pounds (Cal forfeited that bout), had moved up to the higher weight class. Good for him, seemingly very bad for Pat Buzbee who climbed into the ring with him.

BOXING

Sunday, February 13, 1972 | 2 P.M. | CSC North Gym

UNIVERSITY OF CALIF.-BERKELEY	vs.	CHICO STATE COLLEGE
	125 lbs.	forfiet to Chico
Bob Guimarin	132 lbs.	Mike or Pat Buzbee
Larry Wolfe	139 lbs.	John Aceja
Myles O'Dwyer	147 lbs.	John Romero
Pat Kostiz	156 lbs.	Steve Carr
Eric Wolfe	156 lbs.	Tony Ramos
Joe Adams	165 lbs.	Jim Guyn
Chuck Walsh	172 lbs.	Stan Parrish
Scott Stringer	172 lbs.	Ken Kelsch
Ron Frazier	180 lbs.	Des Parrish
Paul Giroday	Heavy.	Rex Montgomery
Stan Stanek	Heavy.	Artie Perez

Referee: Dave Borjon

Judges: Herb Jergentz
Mel Jones
Skip McDonald

Announcer: Bill Wells

Physician: Dr. Maxwell Lee

Timer: Verne Belcher

An *Enterprise-Record* article titled, "CSC Boxers Down Scrappy Cal Bears 7-5," informed readers of a Chico victory, resulting from Wildcats winning seven of fourteen bouts—beginning with Pat Buzbee's victory in the opening match:

> Buzbee opened the card with his 132-pound bout with Bob Guimarin. Guimarin started fast and continually pressed Buzbee in the first round. The Chico Stater began to find the range at the end of the stanzas and hammered away with lefts and rights.
>
> Buzbee continued his attack early in the second round. A hard combination stunned Guimarin and referee Dave Borjon gave the Cal boxer a standing count. That's when Bear coach Nick Carter signaled the fight was over.

1973 CCBC CHAMPIONSHIPS

Material thus far about the Buzbee twins has been devoted to Pat, but he and Mike both represented the Wildcats over the course of each boxing season. Pat later observed about their relative success as pugilists, "Overall, I think Mike did better at boxing than I did. He seemed more resilient than me."

We now jump ahead to the following year, when the 1973 California Collegiate Boxing Conference championships (covering two nights, February 25 and 26) brought that season to a close.

An *E-R* article titled "CCBC Championships Begin Tomorrow Night," served notice that Chico State would enter two boxers in both the 118- and 125-pound weight classes:

> Action begins in the 118-pound division. Chico State has two fighters at that weight. Chuck Avilez battles Nevada-Reno's Jim Jimison in the opener and Pat Buzbee will face the Bears' Andrew Lee in the other.
>
> [Coach Willie] Simmons also has placed two boxers in the 125-pound bracket. Al Castro (2-0) vies with UNR's Jim Morgan and Mike Buzbee will test Cal's Bill Standley.

The article included a photograph of Mike and Pat Buzbee.

Photo 18-3

L-R: Twin brothers Mike and Pat Buzbee.

All four Wildcats fighting at 118 and 125 pounds won their bouts as detailed in the *E-R* under the heading "Cats Dominate First Night of CCBC Tourney:"

> There was action aplenty in the ring last night.
>
> Avilez set the tempo in his fight against UNR's Jim Jimison. Solid left jabs followed by straight rights helped him pound out an easy victory.
>
> Pat Buzbee did not have an easy time in the other 118-pound test. Pat had to come on strong in the final round to edge Cal's Andrew Lee.
>
> Mike Buzbee easily decisioned Cal's Bill Standley. Standley tried to press the issue but landed few punches while Mike unleashed a two-fisted attack throughout each of the three rounds.
>
> Teammate Castro took on UNR's Jim Morgan and maintained his unbeaten status. Referee Bill Moule stopped the fight 50 seconds into the third round as Castro landed straight jabs and hooks at will.

Photo 18-4

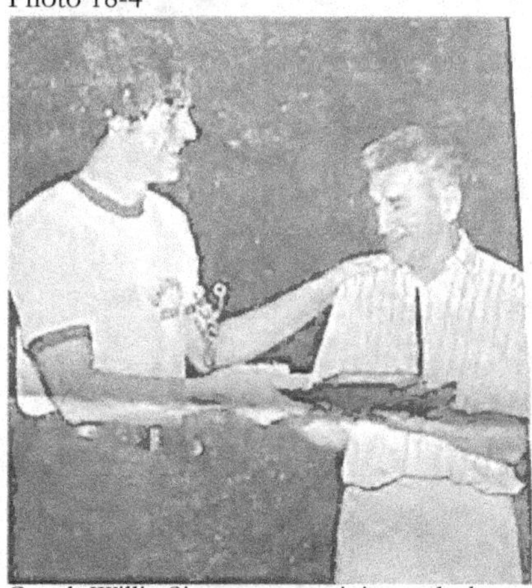

Photo 18-5

Coach Willie Simmons receiving a desk set from University of California Brian Kahn following the California Collegiate Boxing Conference championships. This honor was in appreciation for Simmons' contributions to collegiate boxing. At right is the runner-up trophy earned by Pat Buzbee; Mike also garnered one.

Pat and Mike Buzbee lost their bouts to teammates on the second night of the championship as detailed in the *E-R* under the heading "Eight Wildcats Victorious in CCBC Championships":

> Chico State teammates met in the first two fights. At 118 pounds Chuck Avilez pounded out a unanimous decision over Pat Buzbee.
>
> Avilez took command in the first round with left jabs and hooks. He added enough right-hand follows to keep Buzbee off balance. Buzbee rallied in the second round but when he tried to force the issue in the final canto ran into more jabs and suffered the defeat.
>
> Al Castro (4-0) turned back Mike Buzbee for the 125-pound title. Buzbee was the aggressor throughout the fight but Castro's boxing know-how was the difference. Castro scored with left jabs and hooks to turn the tide and also was able to make Buzbee miss many looping punches.

The fact that four Wildcats contested two final bouts, and that Chico State won eight of ten matches evidenced both the depth and quality of Coach Willie Simmons' boxing program.

Following their college boxing, Pat and Mike Buzbee continued to "take it to the streets" on the road racing circuit in northern California.

Photo 18-6

Photo 18-7

Left: Mike Buzbee handing off to Tracy Smith (world indoor 3-mile record holder) at the 1973 Tahoe Relays. Right: Pat Buzbee finishing in ninth place at the 1977 Avenue of the Giants Marathon in 2:28:43.
Courtesy of Mike and Pat Buzbee

Postscript

Follow your dream. Not the money, but your dream. And never give up. I wanted to be a printmaking professor, but I gave up. Now, I finally get the best of a lot of worlds. As a volunteer teacher, I get to go in every Wednesday morning and help students and I don't have to grade their work.

—My response to Ashley Gebb in 2019 when she asked me,
What advice would you give your graduating self?[1]

Art Shows

Prints of Chico artist Michael Halldorson
Cory's Sweet Treats & Gallery, 230 W. 3rd St.

California State University, Chico *Orion*, November 5, 1997

I could not possibly recount in a single book all the crazy things that I encountered as a naive young man from a small hamlet in northern California. Following graduation from high school and two and a half years of college, I entered the Navy as an immature young man, crazy about rock & roll music—as well as girls, hot rods, and alcohol. As I progressed through my enlistment and gradually grew up, I became more drawn to touring the cities/areas my ship visited, and less to devoting all my time to drinking and chasing girls. I feel that I matured in a way that I might not have, had I not been in the Navy.

Becoming increasingly nostalgic regarding my Navy service, time aboard the *Hopewell*, and of shared experiences with my shipmates, spurred me to author *Navy Daze: Coming of Age in the 1960s Aboard a Navy Destroyer*, published by Heritage Books in 2016. I also remember times of being very homesick and missing my family as one might expect, and of eagerly waiting to get out of the Navy and reenroll in college.

By leaving the service, I was able to return to college and study art under Dr. Janet E. Turner, a printmaker of world renown. I was also able to travel to the Netherlands to spend time with the Dutch graphic artist M. C. Escher—in my estimation, the preeminent printmaker of the 20th Century.

In 2019, I was recipient of the Chico State University distinguished alumni service award for that year. I share this not to be boastful, but instead to make a point. It's possible to take a very long time "coming of age" while seeking adventure and making youthful mistakes, and still eventually become a mature, thoughtful individual. It's also fun to reflect back on the carefree times of one's youth.

Photo Postscript-1

Michael Halldorson's print *Pollution I*, the best print he had done to date as an artist, lying on M. C. Escher's work table. Halldorson presented it to Escher (shown in photo) during a visit to the artist's home in Baarn, Netherlands.

Bibliography/Notes

Bruhn, David D. *Stride Out.* Berwyn Heights, Md: Heritage Books, 2023.

Halldorson, Michael R. *Navy Daze: Coming of Age in the 1960s Aboard a Navy Destroyer.* Berwyn Heights, Md: Heritage Books, 2016.

PREFACE:

[1] Promotional booklet titled "Butte County, California by The Chico Chamber of Commerce, Oroville Chamber of Commerce, Gridley Chamber of Commerce, Biggs Chamber of Commerce, Paradise Progressive Association, Durham Business Men's Association and Richvale Farm Center, 1922" (http://archives.csuchico.edu/digital/collection/coll24/id/60/rec/2: accessed 1 January 2026).
[2] Ibid.
[3] Ibid.
[4] Ibid.
[5] "Hooker Oak" (https://www.hmdb.org/m.asp?m=100595: accessed 2 January 2026).
[6] Promotional booklet titled Butte County, California.
[7] Ibid.
[8] Northeastern California Historical Photograph Collection California State University, Chico (https://calisphere.org/item/d5a93c1e49faccb724cee5afeed81bba/: accessed 2 January 2026).
[9] "A Caduceus History of Chico High School compiled from the volumes of the Chico High Caduceus" by Peter Milbury, C.H.S. Librarian, with contributions from John Nopel (https://chs.chicousd.org/documents/7.%20Departments/Library/A_Caduceus_History_of_Chico_High_School_pdf.pdf: accessed 2 January 2026).
[10] Ibid.
[11] David D. Bruhn, *Stride Out*, Heritage Books, 2023, xv-xvi.
[12] "United States Census data for Chico and Butte, California, from 1850 to 1980" (https://www.dmwilliams.yourweb.csuchico.edu/census/: accessed 2 January 2026).

CHAPTER 1 NOTES:

[1] Michael R. Halldorson, *Navy Daze: Coming of Age in the 1960s Aboard a Navy Destroyer*, Heritage Books, 2016, 1.

CHAPTER 2 NOTES:

[1] "Nelson Briles" by John Stahl (https://sabr.org/bioproj/person/nelson-briles/: accessed January 13, 2026).
[2] Ibid.
[3] Ibid.
[4] Ibid.
[5] Ibid.
[6] Ibid.
[7] Ibid.
[8] Ibid.
[9] Ibid.
[10] Ibid.
[11] Ibid.
[12] Ibid.
[13] Ibid.
[14] Ibid.
[15] Ibid.
[16] Ibid.
[17] Ibid.
[18] Ibid.
[19] Ibid.
[20] Ibid.
[21] Ibid.
[22] Ibid.
[23] Ibid.

CHAPTER 3:

[1] "Cold War relics: Deactivated Titan 1 missile silos surround Beale" (https://www.beale.af.mil/News/Article-Display/Article/280017/cold-war-relics-deactivated-titan-1-missile-silos-surround-beale/: accessed January 18, 2026).
[2] Ibid.
[3] "House of Titans The myths and truths behind Cold War-era missile silos in north Chico" by Tyler Ash (https://www.newsreview.com/chico/content/house-of-titans/13342974/: accessed January 18, 2026).
[4] "Cold War relics: Deactivated Titan 1 missile silos surround Beale;" "House of Titans The myths and truths behind Cold War-era missile silos in north Chico."
[5] "House of Titans The myths and truths behind Cold War-era missile silos in north Chico."
[6] Ibid.
[7] Ibid.
[8] Ibid.
[9] Ibid.
[10] "Cold War relics: Deactivated Titan 1 missile silos surround Beale."

[11] "Cold War relics: Deactivated Titan 1 missile silos surround Beale;" "Missile Silos" (https://localwiki.org/chico/Missile_silos): both accessed January 18, 2026.
[12] Ut supra.
[13] Ut supra.

CHAPTER 4 NOTES:

[1] Chuck Sheley email, 7 January 2026.
[2] Scott Fairley email, 6 January 2026.
[3] Ibid.
[4] Clipping from an unknown newspaper dated May 3, 1963.
[5] Clipping from an unknown newspaper dated May 18, 1963.
[6] "Sig Ohlemann" (https://www.olympedia.org/athletes/66199&lang=en); "Track and Field Statistics" (http://trackfield.brinkster.net/Tournaments.asp?TourCode=P&Year=1963&Gender=M&TF=T&P=F): both accessed 7 January 2026.

CHAPTER 5 NOTES:

[1] "Doug Timmons obituary" (https://www.chicoer.com/obituaries/doug-timmons/: accessed January 27, 2026).
[2] "Timmons: More than 400 Jaguars in 40 years" (https://www.chicoer.com/2009/12/20/timmons-more-than-400-jaguars-in-40-years/: accessed January 27, 2026).
[3] Ibid.
[4] Ibid.
[5] Ibid.

CHAPTER 6 NOTES:

[1] "Silver Dollar Speedway" (https://www.myracepass.com/tracks/1881/news/2025/article/164772/press-release-2025-schedule-is-released: accessed 2 January 2026).
[2] "David Tarter Memorial Race at Chico next up for NARC Sprint Cars on Saturday" (https://narc410.com/2025/06/02/david-tarter-memorial-race-at-chico-next-up-for-narc-sprint-cars-on-saturday/: accessed 3 January 2026).
[3] "Fall Nationals a Tribute to Stephen Allard This Weekend" (https://www.silverdollarspeedway.com/press/2025/article/181677: accessed 3 January 2026).
[4] "(1962-2020) Silver Dollar Speedway 410/360 Sprint Champions" (https://nwsprintcarhistory.com/champions/track-champions/115-california-track-champions/2019-1silver-dollar-speedway-410-sprint-champions: accessed 2 January 2026).
[5] Ibid.
[6] "What Engine Powers a 410 Sprint Car? A Detailed Look at Performance" (https://carxplorer.com/what-engine-is-in-a-410-sprint-car/: accessed 3 January 2026).

[7] "Sprint Car Wings: Aerodynamics for Optimal Performance" (https://www.tibillsraceparts.com/post/sprint-car-wings-aerodynamics-for-optimal-performance: accessed 3 January 2026).

CHAPTER 7 NOTES:

[1] Michael R. Halldorson, *Navy Daze*, 13.
[2] Ibid, 15.
[3] Ibid.
[4] Ibid, 15-16.
[5] Ibid, 16.
[6] Ibid, 16-17.
[7] Ibid, 17.
[8] Ibid.
[9] Ibid.
[10] Ibid, 17-18.
[11] Ibid, 18.
[12] Ibid.
[13] Ibid.
[14] Ibid.

CHAPTER 8 NOTES:

[1] Tim O'Neill email, January 8, 2026.
[2] Sam Simmons email, January 8, 2026.
[3] "Joseph "Rock" McClellan 1921 – 2015" (https://www.legacy.com/us/obituaries/chicoer/name/joseph-mcclellan-obituary?id=37628916); "Clifford 'Blackie' Rowe Gilbert July 19th, 1920 - January 2nd, 2016" (https://www.altogetherfuneral.com/obituaries/d-5418125/chico-california/clifford-rowe-gilbert/january-2016); both accessed January 8, 2026.
[4] Tim O'Neill, email, January 6, 2026.
[5] "1965 Oregon State Beavers Roster" (https://www.sports-reference.com/cfb/schools/oregon-state/1965-roster.html: accessed January 8, 2026).
[6] "Pete Pifer" (https://en.wikipedia.org/wiki/Pete_Pifer: accessed January 9, 2026).

CHAPTER 9 NOTES:

[1] "Powell Rods Company" (https://powellco.com/pages/company); "E. C. Powell" (https://classicpowellrod.com/e-c-powell): both accessed 5 January 2026).
[2] Ut supra.
[3] "Walton Powell" (https://classicpowellrod.com/walton-powell); "Spare the rod" (https://www.newsreview.com/chico/content/spare-the-rod/5239/): both accessed 5 January 2026.
[4] "Spare the rod."
[5] Ibid.

[6] "Phillip Press Powell Obituary" (https://www.legacy.com/us/obituaries/chicoer/name/phillip-powell-obituary?id=27403910: accessed 6 January 2026).
[7] Ibid.
[8] California State University, Chico *Orion*, "Fly-fishing skills easier to manage than catching fish," October 6, 1999; California State University, Chico *Orion*, "Casting Illusion," September 29, 1993.
[9] Tim O'Neill email, 6 January 2026.
[10] Ibid.

CHAPTER 10 NOTES:

[1] Michael R. Halldorson, *Navy Daze*, 53.
[2] Ibid, 43.
[3] Ibid.
[4] Ibid, 71.
[5] Ibid, 72.
[6] Ibid, 74.
[7] Ibid.

CHAPTER 11 NOTES:

[1] *Chico Enterprise-Record* "Schools Open Today Enrollment Up Slightly," September 7, 1965.
[2] Ibid.
[3] "Laxson Auditorium" (https://www.csuchico.edu/upe/venues/laxson.shtml: accessed 4 January 2026).
[4] Rob Laxson email, 6 January 2026.
[5] "Melvin Dalrymple Obituary" (https://www.legacy.com/us/obituaries/chicoer/name/melvin-dalrymple-obituary?id=17027829: accessed 4 January 2026).
[6] Ibid.
[7] Ibid.
[8] Ibid.
[9] "Hall of Fame Team 1967 Giant Killers" (https://d3164imkzcru7c.cloudfront.net/honors/hall-of-fame/team--giant-killers/141: accessed 3 January 2026).
[10] "Hall of Fame Team 1967 Giant Killers;" Rob Laxson email, 3 January 2026.
[11] "1967 USC at Oregon State" (https://www.youtube.com/watch?v=1jl0YxkoTGU: accessed 3 January 2026).
[12] "Hall of Fame Team 1967 Giant Killers;" "1967 All-Pacific-8 Conference football team" (https://americanfootballdatabase.fandom.com/wiki/1967_All-Pacific-8_Conference_football_team); "1966 Oregon State Beavers Roster" (https://www.sports-reference.com/cfb/schools/oregon-state/1966-

roster.html); "1967 Oregon State Beavers Roster" (https://www.sports-reference.com/cfb/schools/oregon-state/1967-roster.html): all accessed 6 January 2026.
[13] "Gary Houser" (https://www.profootballarchives.com/players/h/hous00550.html: accessed 6 January 2026).
[14] "Gary Houser retiring after 15 years as Shasta College AD" (https://archive.redding.com/news/gary-houser-retiring-after-15-years-as-shasta-college-ad-ep-299130538-353604721.html: accessed 4 January 2026).
[15] Chico State College *Wildcat*, May 5, 1969.
[16] Ibid.

CHAPTER 12 NOTES:

[1] Michael R. Halldorson, *Navy Daze*, 101.
[2] Ibid, 118.
[3] Ibid.
[4] Ibid.
[5] Ibid, 119.
[6] Ibid.
[7] Ibid.

CHAPTER 13 NOTES:

[1] Michael R. Halldorson, *Navy Daze*, 120.
[2] Ibid, 120-121.
[3] Ibid, 122.
[4] Ibid.
[5] Ibid, 122-123.
[6] Ibid, 123.
[7] Ibid.
[8] Ibid, 124.

CHAPTER 14 NOTES:

[1] "Did the news media, led by Walter Cronkite, lose the war in Vietnam" (https://www.washingtonpost.com/national/did-the-news-media-led-by-walter-cronkite-lose-the-war-in-vietnam/2018/05/25/a5b3e098-495e-11e8-827e-190efaf1f1ee_story.html?utm_term=.da9a56dfd832: accessed 2 December 2018).
[2] "Vietnam War Campaigns" (https://history.army.mil/html/reference/army_flag/vn.html: accessed 19 October 2018).
[3] "Did the news media, led by Walter Cronkite, lose the war in Vietnam."
[4] *Chico Enterprise-Record*, February 29, 1968 (https://exhibits.csuchico.edu/files/original/2e194ecd8a9741c66d8e923f22509411a8857f9e.jpg: accessed January 21, 2026).
[5] "It was a gas Chico's purple haze of music and politics in 1968" by Alan Sheckter, *Chico News and Review*, July 17, 2008

(https://www.newsreview.com/chico/content/it-was-a-gas/694453/: accessed January 20, 2026).
[6] Chico State College *Wildcat*, May 27, 1970.

CHAPTER 15 NOTES:

[1] Sam Simmons email, January 21, 2026.
[2] "It was a gas Chico's purple haze of music and politics in 1968."
[3] Ibid.
[4] Chico State College *Wildcat*, January 5, 1968.
[5] "Rawls, Louis Allen, SGT" (https://army.togetherweserved.com/army/servlet/tws.webapp.webapp?cmd=ShadowBoxProfile&type=Person&ID=343131&binder=true: accessed January 20, 2026).
[6] Ibid.
[7] "What Happened To The Members Of The Fifth Dimension" (https://inckredible.com/what-happened-to-the-members-of-the-fifth-dimension/: accessed January 20, 2026).
[8] Ibid.
[9] "Big Brother and the Holding Company" (https://www.classicrockconnection.com/main/big-brother-and-the-holding-company/: accessed January 20, 2026).
[10] Ibid.
[11] Ibid.
[12] "It was a gas Chico's purple haze of music and politics in 1968."
[13] Ibid.
[14] Ibid.
[15] Chico State College *Wildcat*, February 10, 1969.
[16] Ibid.

CHAPTER 16 NOTES:

[1] "It was a gas Chico's purple haze of music and politics in 1968."
[2] Michael R. Halldorson, *Navy Daze*, 125-126.
[3] Ibid.
[4] Bill Gregg email, January 19, 2026.

CHAPTER 17 NOTES:

[1] "Garth H. Dunning obituary" (https://www.findagrave.com/memorial/64521371/garth_h-dunning); "PE department hit by summer tragedy," Chico State College *Wildcat*, September 17, 1969): both accessed 16 January 2026.
[2] Ibid.
[3] "Chico State Athletic Hall of Fame" (https://chicowildcats.com/documents/2012/4/19/1987_Hall_of_Fame.pdf?id=1468: accessed 16 January 2026).

CHAPTER 18 NOTES:

[1] "William Simmons Obituary" (https://www.legacy.com/us/obituaries/chicoer/name/william-simmons-obituary?id=15572514: accessed January 9, 2026).

[2] "'Greatest athlete to ever put on a Chico State uniform,' Maderos dies at 83" (https://www.chicoer.com/2017/02/03/greatest-athlete-to-ever-put-on-a-chico-state-uniform-maderos-dies-at-83/: accessed January 9, 2026).

POSTSCRIPT NOTE:

[1] "5 Questions with Distinguished Alumnus Michael Halldorson," Chico State Today (https://today.csuchico.edu/5-questions-with-distinguished-alumnus-michael-halldorson/: accessed January 27, 2026).

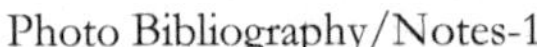

Photo Bibliography/Notes-1

Michael Halldorson's print titled *Pollution I* (introduced on page 96) was inspired by Earth Day in 1970, and his desire to highlight the ill effects of, and need to combat pollution. Sources of pollution in the print include smoke from a logging yard beehive burner, train locomotives, and factory smoke stacks. The gas mask and elevator suggest that given no dramatic reduction of pollution, mankind might have to wear protective gear or live below the earth's surface.

About the Author

Michael R. Halldorson enlisted in the Naval Reserve in 1961, at age eighteen. Following two-and-a-half years of college, he went on active duty, serving aboard the destroyer USS *Hopewell* (DD-681) during two deployments to the Western Pacific, which included combat duty in the waters off Vietnam.

After leaving active duty, he returned to college and studied art while concurrently being a member of the Naval Reserve. Halldorson graduated in 1969 with a BA Degree in Art, and promptly entered the management side of his family's business.

In ensuing years, he pursued graduate studies in art, while juggling family, business, professional artist, and Naval Reserve duty obligations. Halldorson is currently a board member of the Janet Turner Art Museum, housed within California State University, Chico; and a member of the Chico Rotary Club, and other civic and veterans' organizations.

He is most proud of serving as the commander of VFW Post 1555, a position his father—who fought in World War II and was a POW in Germany—held fifty years ago. Halldorson grew up around VFW activities, and considers it a great honor to continue the legacy of the late TSgt Magnus Michael Halldorson, United States Army.

(Photograph provided courtesy of Michelle Camy.)

About the Author

Commander David D. Bruhn, U.S. Navy (Retired) served twenty-two years on active duty and two in the Naval Reserve, as both an enlisted man and as an officer, between 1977 and 2001.

He is a graduate of California State University, Chico, and has Masters degrees from the U.S. Naval Postgraduate School and U.S. Naval War College.

During his career, Bruhn served aboard six ships including command of the mine countermeasures ships USS *Gladiator* (MCM-11) and USS *Dextrous* (MCM-13) in the Persian Gulf. Ashore, he did two three-year tours in the Pentagon. During the first one, he was assigned to Secretary of the Navy and Chief of Naval Operation staffs as a budget analyst and resources planner. His final assignment was to the Secretary of Defense staff as executive assistant to a senior (SES 4) executive at the Ballistic Missile Defense Organization in Washington, D.C.

Following military service, he was a high school teacher and track coach for ten years, and remains an avid Track & Field fan. He lives in northern California with his wife Nancy and has two grown sons, David and Michael.

Bruhn has authored thirty-six books, which include 28 on naval history, 1 on army hospital ships, and 1 on shipboard engineering. In other subjects, there are 4 related to sports—*Toe the Mark*, *Stride Out*, *Distant Finish*, and *Beavers* about competitive running in the 1970s—1 about building a mahogany plywood camper for a lightweight truck, titled *Land Yacht Seaward*; and 1 about creating a British pub in a garage, titled *Stand Easy* (meaning take a break).

www.ingramcontent.com/pod-product-compliance
Lightning Source LLC
LaVergne TN
LVHW020634100826
845148LV00012B/2179